IT´S LOGICAL!

D1263479

Rodopi Philosophical Studies

4

Edited by

Francisco Miró Quesada
(University of Lima)

Ernest Sosa
(Brown University)

Amsterdam - Atlanta, GA 1999

Katalin G. Havas

IT´S LOGICAL!

∞ The paper on which this book is printed meets the requirements of "ISO 9706:1994, Information and documentation - Paper for documents - Requirements for permanence".

ISBN: 90-420-0497-5
©Editions Rodopi B.V., Amsterdam - Atlanta, GA 1999
Printed in The Netherlands

CONTENTS

I.

What is it good for?

M. Jourdain, Moliere's self-made gentleman asks the 'philosophy master' to write a love letter to his sweetheart in his name. When the 'master' asks whether the letter should be written in verse or prose, the dialogue goes on like this:

"M. Jourdain. No. I don't want either verse or prose.
Philosophy Master. But it must be one or the other.
I. Jourdain. Why?
Philosophy Master. Because, Monsieur, there are only two ways of expressing oneself, in prose or in verse.
II. Jourdain. There's nothing except prose or verse?
Philosophy Master. No, Monsieur. Whatever is not prose is verse, and whatever is not verse is prose.
III. Jourdain. What is ordinary speech then?
Philosophy Master. Prose.
IV. Jourdain. What! When I say: 'Nicole, fetch me my slippers, and give me my nightcap', is that prose?
Philosophy Master. Yes, Monsieur.
V. Jourdain. Good Heavens! Then I have been speaking prose for more than forty years without knowing it. I couldn't be more grateful to you for teaching me that".

If we ask laymen to tell what logical operations they use when they solve a problem, it is highly probable that they would have difficulty answering just as the self-made gentleman did not know he was speaking in prose. In spite of the fact that they usually think according to some kind of logical principles they are not familiar with any logical theories.

A person with an acute logical faculty might not be aware of the rules of logic, just as an excellent housewife might not be able to tell the exact dosage of spices she uses to season her cooking so marvelously. If we asked her answer would be:

"I do not know the proportions, but I taste the food until it tastes good. Why do I use this stuff? I have learned it from my mother. I have always done it this way, and it works. But to tell the truth, I know little about the characteristics of the stuff I use."

But occasionally our housewife may wish to look at a good cookbook. Not because she does not know how to cook without it, but because she wants to improve her knowledge of cooking or to give it variety. Perhaps she wants to explore other recipes, or make her work easier or quicker. Or, perhaps, she needs to use a cookbook because this time she has to make dinner for a lot of people, and although she knows that she has to put a handful of rice and a touch of salt in the stuffed cabbage for her family, she does not know how much to use for 150 people.

The cookbook is, of course, only an aid; it is not enough in itself to prepare a tasty meal. Good raw materials are needed as well as the skill and experience of the housewife. But the knowledge of recipes is also a useful aid in her work.

The success of cognition depends on a number of factors besides logical thinking. It depends on the so-called background knowledge, that is, on the amount of knowledge of the contemporary historical period, and especially on what one knows at the moment when the performance of the logical operation begins.

Logical studies are not concerned with these other factors. They are not concerned with where a man has acquired the knowledge which is the prerequisite of making logical operations; nor are they concerned whether or not this knowledge consists of the tenets of some advanced science or simply refers to the rules of a game. Logic as a science is concerned with the problem of how new knowledge can be acquired from given knowledge, merely by way of reasoning.

We have become used to asking the questions: 'What is the use of it? What is it good for?' And you have probably asked yourselves:

Of what use is it to Moliere's 'self-made gentleman' to know that he speaks in prose?

Similarly, the question may be raised, what is the knowledge of the rules of logic good for if we can think correctly without knowing them?

I have to answer, first, that although it is important to look for practical applications, this is not the only reason why a man may wish to acquire knowledge. Just remember that even a little child wishes to know the „why's". We generally scold the little girl who takes her doll apart in order to see what is inside, or the boy, who does the same with his toy car. They are driven by natural curiosity, the desire for knowledge. In this way the desire for knowledge in itself would justify our occupation with the laws of logic. But this is not all we are talking about. We can make use of the knowledge of logic. It promotes the development of logical thinking and especially the discovery of logical errors.

The long-distance runner can run well without knowing the physical and psychological processes which take place in running, and surely he is a better runner than the aged professor, who knows all these processes well. But for the runner knowing them is a great help in improving his technique, and is a great help as well for his trainer, for the person who teaches him how to run, who wants to correct his errors and eliminate his shortcomings.

II.

Have you any idea of it?

One day Vera told me she wanted to become a scholar.

"Have you any idea of how much a scholar has to learn?" I asked her.

"No" she said, a little sadly. "I don't even know when we can say that we have an idea of something, or that we have not the slightest idea."

"Well, let us begin the 'training of the scholar' right now. Let us talk about ideas, or to be more precise, let's talk about one of the meanings of the word idea. For this meaning logic uses the word 'concept'."

"When we have a concept of something, we know what the characteristics are by which we can separate it and distinguish it from other things."

"You have used a number of words that are no more familiar to me than the word 'concept' is. Would you be so kind and explain them? First of all, what does 'characteristics' mean?"

"The properties of a thing, and its relation to other things are called the characteristics of a thing.
Each thing has a number of properties and has relations to the other things that are different."

"What do you mean by properties?"

"A certain coat, for example, is brown, is made of balloon-cloth, has a stain on it, and so on. These are its properties."

"And what does relation mean?"

"You see, if this coat - which is brown and made of balloon-cloth and has a stain on it, etc. - belongs to inspector Colombo, this coat is characterized by its relationship to inspector Colombo."

"I think that characteristics can not exist without the thing which they characterize. The color 'brown' exists together with the thing which is brown, and a grin exists together with that which is grinning."

"Yes, and a relationship can't exist without the things that are related. How did this idea come to your mind?"

"Don't you remember? I read about it in my favorite story-book a long time ago. You know, the book you too like so much because it was written by a professor of logic, and he worked all sorts of logical problems into the story."

"Oh, I see! Where does Lewis Carroll speak of this idea?"

"Alice asked the Cheshire Cat not to keep appearing and vanishing so suddenly because it made her quite giddy. This time the Cat vanished quite slowly, beginning with the end of its tail, and ending with the grin. But the grin remained for some time after the rest of it had gone. Alice thought she had seen a cat without a grin, but she had never seen a grin without a cat.

"Of course she had not, because this is possible only in Wonderland.

In reality no characteristic can exist without the thing to which it belongs, but various things may have the same characteristics. It is not only the coat, for example, which may be brown, but a ribbon and a piece of furniture as well.

It is the properties and the relations on the basis of which we can include things in a class (for example, *'brown things'*) and on the basis of which we can distinguish them from one another (for example, *'brown things'* and *'not-brown things'*). When we form a concept of something we include it in a class of things on the basis of its some characteristics, that is, we identify it with things which also have the same characteristics. In this way we may obtain concepts like *'metal object'*, *'mammal'*, *'game'*. Individual metal objects, thus for example, *'iron objects'*, *'copper objects'*, etc., constitute the extension of the concept of *'metal object'*. The group of characteristics which can be found in every metal object and on the basis of which we form a class, constitute the intension of a concept. The intension of a concept is a group of certain characteristics. When it serves to express a concept, the word *'mammal'* denotes one of the animals which we rank with the mammals on the basis of certain of its characteristics.

"This is a little difficult for me. Later I will probably understand it better."

"I hope so. We will speak about it several times. But now let us turn back to the characteristics of concepts."

When-forming a concept, in a way we become detached from what appears in the sensual image of the object. But this detachment makes better recognition of the object possible. We can recognize those characteristics of the object which can not be sensed directly through concept formation. Besides things that can be sensed, we can form concepts of things which can not be perceived by the senses. Contrary to sensual recognition, conceptual cognizance makes us recognize not only material objects which extend in space and time. We are able to form concepts of objects which do not exist in the present, but existed only in the past, or will exist in the future. Besides individual objects we can form concepts of groups of objects, of the characteristics and relationships of objects, etc. We can even form concepts of objects which do not exist in the material world."

"Does this mean that we recognize essences through concepts?"

"It is usually said that in a concept the object is reflected through its essential characteristics. When I see an object, I see that it is cylinder-like, is made of glass, has cracks in it, is decorated with drawings, is on my desk, and so on. But when I think of this object as the *only memento I have inherited from my grandmother*', I stress, as it is said, it's essential characteristic, and disregard such inessential characteristics of the given thing as, for example, there being cracks in it. But the 'essence' of a given thing depends on how we relate to it in our thoughts. This thing is not only a *'memento'*, but also a *'drinking-glass'*. As a drinking-glass its essence is different. But when I think of this object as the only memento in my room, its essential characteristic will be something other than *'drinking-glass'*."

"Please, wait a little while I fetch my book *The Little Prince*. I remember a passage which says that essence means something quite different for adults than for children. I will look it up and read it. Here it is! Listen!"

> "'If I told you these details about the asteroid, and made a note of its number for you, it is on account of the grown-ups and their ways. Grown-ups love figures. When you tell them that you have made a new friend, they never ask you any questions about essential matters. They never say to you, 'What does his voice sound like? What games does he love best? Does he collect butterflies?' Instead, they demand: 'How old is he? How many brothers has he? How much does

he weigh? How much money does his father make?' Only from these figures do they think they have learned anything about him."

Vera sat in silence for a time after she had finished reading. She seemed to be lost in her thoughts. Then she said:

"If essence is different for different people, if essence is different in different relationships, can we say that there is something among the *'essentials'* which is the *'most essential'*? Is there such a thing?"

"Up to this date philosophers have given debatable answers to this question. Therefore we better avoid the word *'essence'*, and say: concepts reflect things only in some aspects, on the basis of some characteristics. No one concept can reproduce the thing in its completeness, in respect to all of its properties and relations."

"You use the word *'thing'* many times, what do you mean by it?"

"You already know that not only material objects can be reflected in concepts. Therefore I call a *'thing'* everything that we can imagine or think about."

"I do not regard this term to be very good, but other terms I could propose, such as *'something'*, *'anything'*, *'thingamajig'* are by no means more expressive. But let's turn back to concepts!"

"I would like to talk some more about the relationship between words and concepts."

"Oh, this is especially interesting for me, because perhaps I will become a linguist!"

"The word or a group of words is the linguistic form of expressing a concept. For example, *'man'* is a concept expressed in one word, and *'electrical conductor'* is a concept expressed in a group of words. Every concept is expressed in words but not all words express concepts."

"Yes, I know. Even some words by which we merely express feelings do not express concepts. For example, *'oh'*, *'ouch'*, *'well'*."

"You will learn that there are words which are the linguistic expressions of logical operations performed with concepts or propositions. For example, in the sentence *'Today it is cold and the sun is shining'* the word *'and'* is used to connect propositions.

It is usually the common name which expresses a concept. It is a name which can be applied to all members of a given class and which expresses the common characteristics of the elements of the given class on the basis of what we have thought of the elements of the given class. For example, we could designate every individual which belongs to the class of men as man, we could designate a triangle all three sides of which are equal as 'equilateral triangle', and every planet which belongs to the solar system as 'planet of the solar system', etc.

We can use several words to express the same concept. 'rhombus' and 'equilateral quadrangle' are the linguistic expressions of the same concept. The word 'rhombus' can be considered as a shorter expression of the already existing term, 'equilateral quadrangle'."

"When I know the name of something, can I be sure that I have a concept of it?"

"No, not at all. We may know the name of something even when we have not the slightest idea of the thing which is called by that name. 'He is just talking without having any idea of what he is talking about' - we say when somebody uses certain terms without knowing what they mean."

"I think that now I have some idea of the meaning of 'concept'."

"Yes, you already know that it is the thought content of certain words, that it serves to reflect an object in the mind through characteristics that belong only to that object."

"Is this knowledge enough to say that I have formed a concept of 'concept'?"

"Yes. But if you know only this much of 'concept', you are only at the beginning of getting to know it. Often it is only preliminary knowledge, when we know the characteristics by which we can separate objects from one another. In this case we only know what it is we want to get to know later. These so-called 'preliminary concepts' characterize an early stage of the process of cognition. The further task of cognition is to enrich the concept of an object through the knowledge of more and more characteristics. For example, a student has a concept of magnetism, and so does the tailor who uses a magnet to pick-up pins, as well as a physicist. Yet their concepts differ from one another according to the extent of their knowledge. Therefore I propose to continue our discourse about 'concepts' the next time."

Let's play 'Bar Kochba'!

"Today we will play 'Bar Kochba'. As you will see this game enables you to get to know the characteristics of concepts better."

"I don't know this game. Please, tell me how to play it."

"'Bar Kochba' is very similar to the game 'Twenty questions' which I am sure you know. Bar Kochba was the Hebrew leader of a revolt against Rome (in 135). He sent a scout to the Roman camp. The scout was captured, brutally tortured, even his tongue was ripped out. Later he managed to escape and returned to Bar Kochba. As he was unable to speak, Bar Kochba learned what he had seen in the Roman Camp by asking him questions which could be answered by yes and no. The soldier gave the answer by nodding or shaking his head. In this way Bar Kochba got to know everything he wanted to know from the scout.

We don't know whether or not this is a true story. Maybe it was invented by the person who invented the game; and we don't even know who this person might be. To be sure, the game was very popular in Budapest already at the beginning of the twentieth century. Prominent writers were enthusiastic players of this game and they mention it in some of their works.

The game goes as follows:

> *The players form two sides. One side, usually a group or a single person, must decide on something (living being, lifeless thing, concept). The other side, usually a single person, has to find out what this thing is by asking question. He has to formulate the questions in such a way that they could be answered with 'yes' or 'no'. The informants have to answer every question and give a true answer. The game ends when the questioner names the thing that had to be guessed."*

"Let's begin to play!"

"I will ask the questions, and you, Vera, will answer me."

"Is it a living being?"

"Yes."

"A plant?"

"No."

"A mammal?"

"Yes."

"A domesticated animal?"

"No."

"A placental animal?"

"No."

"Oviparous?"

"Yes."

"Does it have a bill?"

"Yes."

"I already know!"

"Then tell me, please."

"It is a duckbill."

"Yes. How did you find it out so quickly?"

"When I asked the questions I asked about the characteristics of that which I had to guess. When you said 'yes' I knew that what I have to guess belongs to the class of things which has the given characteristics. I knew that each characteristic for which your answer was 'yes' is common to many kinds of living beings. But the only living being which is a mammal, oviparous and has a bill, is the duckbill. These characteristics together constitute the content of the concept of duckbill.

But I have to admit that I can't always find out everything so quickly. When you said 'yes' to the question 'mammal', I guessed what you had thought of. I know that yesterday, when you worked on a crossword puzzle, you came across the information: 'the duckbill is like that'. You looked in the lexicon and found the solution oviparous. You said you were surprised to know that such an animal should exist. I supposed that you had this idea in the back of your mind, and my supposition was correct."

"The next time I will give you a more difficult problem."

"When a player has little knowledge about the thing he has to find out, it becomes more difficult."

"The day before yesterday I did not know that there are three classes of mammals: oviparous, marsupial and placental. Had I been the guesser at that time I should have had difficulties in asking my questions."

"Oh yes. Often you can hear the guesser ask himself: 'What should I ask next?'

When you have no knowledge about the concrete characteristics of the thing you have to guess, logic can not help you. But it can when it points to possible questions which, whatever the thing to be guessed may be, can help you. I will mention a few questions of this kind, if you wish, and explain the correct answers for you."

"I will be pleased to listen to it."

Is it one individual thing?

To this question the answer is yes when the totality of the characteristics apply to one individual thing that has to be guessed. The concept which corresponds to it is called an **individual concept**. An individual concept may be, for example, *'prime number between 2 and 4'*. Similarly *'capital of Hungary'* is also an individual concept. It is the linguistic expression of a thing considered on the basis of some characteristics. The extension of an individual concept is a class of one element.

We produce an individual concept by stressing certain characteristics which a given thing possessed at different times and by abstracting others from among these characteristics. Thus the individual concept is also the result of generalization, of abstraction.

"And if I would use the word *'Budapest'* instead of *'capital of Hungary'*? Is *'Budapest'* also an expression of a concept?"

"It's a good question. In some cases it is but in some other cases it is not."

"What do you mean?"

"The word Budapest may function as a linguistic abbreviation for *'capital of Hungary'*, in this case it expresses a concept. But in some other cases *'Budapest'*, just like other proper names as Mercury, Moon, does not express a concept. Proper names usually denote definite objects which are not generalized as elements of a class. However, concepts exist only through generalization.

But I can see that you want to ask something. Go on!"

"Yes. When you mentioned Mercury and Moon I began to wonder if *'solar system'* is a certain thing, or not? Is this also an individual concept?"

"That's also a good question. We shall analyze it. But before doing so I would like to tell you a few words about **general concepts**."

"Go on!"

"When it is *'bus ticket'*, *'rattle'* or *'duckbill'* that you have to guess, the correct answer is that it is not one certain thing, because the totality of the characteristics which constitute the content of the concept can refer to a number of things. These are general concepts. When it is a general concept you have to guess, we can say *'yes'* to the questions referring to the characteristics of any of the bus tickets, rattles or duckbills. When using a general concept we are thinking of one thing, but this one thing can be any one of the things which constitute the extension of the concept.

Now, please tell me if there are several things you can call solar system?"

"No, I don't thing so. But, but, ... Wait a minute! We have just learned in school that the solar system consists of the Sun and the complex assemblage of bodies, gas and dust bound to it by gravitation..."

"Yes, but the characteristics of the solar system are not characteristics of the individual components which belong to it. If you have to guess *'solar system'*, the answer is *'yes'* to the question whether there are nine known major planets in it, but you can not say the same of the planet Mercury. I.e. the extension of the concept *'solar system'* does not include several things of which you can call *'solar system'*. This is not the case with the concept *'bus ticket'*, the extension of which includes several things which you can call *'bus ticket'*.

'Solar system' is a **collective concept**, like for example, the concept *'family'*. *'Family'* is a **general collective concept**. There are different families and each of them consist of members; mother, father, daughter, etc. But, what you can tell about a family as a whole, you can not tell about the separate members of the family. I.e. the characteristics of a family are not characteristics of the members of the family.

The things which comprise the extension of a collective concept are themselves groups of different things.

In the extension of *'solar system'* there is only one group of things and we think about this one group of things as one thing. That is why 'solar system' is an **individual collective concept**.
Was I able to convince you?"

"H'm, h'm... Not really, because you cut me short. I wanted to tell you, we had learned in school that the uniqueness of the solar system is questioned."

"But this is another story! You changed the subject, as it is often done by somebody who refuses to recognize her mistake."

"No, no! I only wanted to ask how would it be if we found out, in the future, that there are many solar system?"

"In this case our *'solar system'* concept would be changed and what I told you would be valid only about our solar system. Our solar system would be one of the members of the class of solar system."

"Oh, I see! Would you tell in this case that *'solar system'* is a general collective concept?"

"You are very clever! That would be the case. It would be a general collective concept like 'family', or 'wood' or 'nation', etc.
Now it is your turn to tell me why *'wood'*, *'nation'* are collective concepts?"

"I know, the characteristics of wood are characteristics of the different woods but they are not characteristics of the trees, bushes, etc. which consist of wood. And in the same way what ever you can say about a nation you can't say about a member of that nation i.e. about a person."

Is it an existing or imaginary thing?

"The philosophers of the ancient world had already raised the question whether things which correspond to general concepts exist in reality or are only the products of our minds. As an old story says, a philosopher asked his friend to bring him some fruit. When brought a pear, the philosopher said: 'I did not ask you for a pear, I asked you for some fruit'. His friend had to admit that he was unable to bring him fruit as such, fruit in the general sense, but only pear, apple, plum, and so on. But could not even bring him pear in the general sense, only white butter-pear, butter-pear, and so on. But could not even bring white butter-pear in general, only the one, which for example, grew on the highest branch of the furthermost tree in the garden."

"But do white butter pear, pear and fruit not exist?"

"Yes, they do: as the common characteristics of several, different things. In the same manner - although each individual love is different - there exists love in reality, and unfortunately, there exists gossip, alcoholism, etc.

In contrast, we have concepts possessing characteristics, - which constitute their contents - that do not refer to any actually existing thing. These are called **empty concepts**. Thus, for example, *'the present King of France'*, *'perpetual motion object'* are empty concepts.

As regards empty concepts we may raise the question whether these concepts can be considered reflections of reality. The answer is yes they are the products of such reflections. The outside world is not reflected in concepts exactly the same way as a thing can be seen in a mirror. When reflecting the world in concepts we separate characteristics which appear together in reality, and we link characteristics conceptually which can not be found together in a single, actually existing thing. But the basis, the starting point of this mental activity is acquired knowledge of the characteristics of existing things through the cognition of reality.

It was man who, for example, created the empty concepts of *'giant'*, *'dwarf'*, *'the land of giants'*, *'the land of dwarfs'* as the imitations of earthly things. In the real world Swift's land of giants and land of dwarfs do not exist. But there exist things in the real world which might give a basis for the imagination to create such concepts. People once believed in the existence of the philosopher's stone which changes everything into gold, and they once believed in the negative weight of phlogiston which is given off by anything burning. Only in the course of the progress of knowledge did it become clear that the extension of these concepts is empty. We can not say, however, that every empty concept is the result of the false reflection of reality.

The truth is that science could not progress without creating empty concepts. Man has created the concept of *'steam engine'*, *'satellite'* before he could produce it in reality. At the time of their inception these concepts were empty, but they were based on things which already existed in reality and they made it possible to produce objects which at first existed only conceptually. In sciences concepts are often used without knowing whether they are empty or not. Scientists need them for creating hypotheses. That is the case with the concept of other solar systems beside ours, which you have mentioned."

Abstract concept?

"Before examining this question I show you a list which I compiled from the problems of some Bar Kochba games I have played earlier.

Living being:
   Blue bird, Noe (from the Bible).
Lifeless thing:
   Desdemona's handkerchief (in Shakespeare's Othello),
   diaper, bus ticket,   baby's rattle.
Concept:
   Mephistophelean laughter, gossip, love, house-party,
   Gulliver's travels, goal, carnival time, alcoholism, equality of
   rights.

You can see from this list that the term 'concept' is used in different sense in Bar Kochba than in logic.
This is permissible. We can reach a tacit understanding in every game which is valid only within the framework of the game."

"But it is unfortunate that we can not find detailed instructions for use anywhere."

"Yes it is. But what are we to do? Let's try to find out what 'concept' means in Bar Kochba!"

"I think the things which belong to the category of concept in Bar Kochba are not tangible things. Or to put it more precisely, they can not exist independently in space, that is, they denote characteristics of relations of objects or living beings, or they denote events. In short, in Bar Kochba we range within the category of concept everything we do not think of as a lifeless thing or living being existing in time or space."

"You are more or less right. At least I think so. But first let's see what we are looking for in Bar Kochba. It is important to see it clearly. When you are looking for something, the first requirement is to know wnat you are looking for. That is, you have to understand your task. This applies to problems of production, to solving mathematical problems and to answering scientific questions, and this also applies to logical games."

"It is clear to me. In Bar Kochba we always have to guess a thing conceived in its conceptual form; it may be a living being, a lifeless object or a concept, which we ascertain from the 'yes' answers at the outset of the game."

"Do we ask for a living being? But Bar Kochba is not a game like hide-and-seek, where you have to find a person. And in the 'fire-water' game we are looking for a material object. Here the task is to really find a hidden object on the basis of information received from the players, who indicate the proximity of the object by saying *'water'*, *'lukewarm'*, *'warm'*, *'hot'*, *'fire'*."

"Do we always look for a concept then?"

"This is nearer to the truth, but it involves a number of problems."

"I feel that way too. If the objective in every case is to find out a concept, why does the informant say 'no' in some instances to the question *'is it a concept?'* Why are three categories? If, for example, we have to guess *'Desdemona's handkerchief'*, the informant will say *'yes'* to the question *'is it a material thing?'* while the correct answer to the question *'Is it a concept?'* is *'no'*."

"That's right. I can say that in Bar Kochba the objective is to find a thing reflected in conceptual form. We do not look for the thing itself, or for the concept itself, but for the thing as it appears in a concept."

"Could somebody say that the objective is not to find a living being, a thing or a concept, but rather, a word or group of words?"

"Yes, perhaps. However I do not like this statement. If the objective is to find out the word *'vase'*, how can we say *'yes'* to the question *'can it be filled with water'*?"

"That is right. There is no word which we can fill with water. Words can contain thoughts, they can contain letters, but can never contain water."

"Therefore in Bar Kochba the objective is not to recognize a word or a group of words on the basis of the characteristics of a word or a group of words. (Although sometimes it is possible that what we have to find out, for example, *'the words in the English orthographical dictionary'* belongs to the realm of words).

Do you accept that it is not the word but, rather, what it denotes, that we ask for in Bar Kochba?

"Yes, I do, but I do not know whether the two affirmations, that we ask for a thing reflected in conceptual form and we ask for a thing denoted by a word, do not contradict each other."

"In these two affirmations we speak about a thing in different relationships, first in its relationship to a concept, then in its relationship to linguistic expression."

"Is it correct if I say: in Bar Kochba we have to guess a thing we have imagined in the form of a concept and which is denoted by a word?"

"Yes, it is."

"Are we now nearer to find out what does 'concept' mean in Bar Kochba?"

"Yes, I think we are.

Regarding the categories of 'living being' and 'lifeless thing ' you have to guess an object imagined in the form of concrete concept, while the category of concept refers to objects which make up the extension of abstract concepts.

A **concrete concept** may include one or more objects or groups of objects, one or more living beings or groups of living beings which we have selected from among lifeless objects or living beings on the basis of certain characteristics.

Abstract concept is the result of mental activity in the course of which we detach the characteristics from the things which have them, and subsequently, we think not of the objects as bearers of these characteristics, but the characteristics themselves, independent of what object or objects possess them. The extension of the abstract concept includes characteristics. For example, the concept of *'color'* includes colors such as white, green, yellow, and so on.

'Gossip' is an abstract concept as opposed to the concrete concept of *'gossiper'*. *'Love'* is also an abstract concept as opposed to the concrete concept of *'lover'*. A lover has different characteristics than love does. A lover is a person, therefore he or she can walk

absentmindedly along the street, but love cannot do that. If *'love'* is to be guessed the answer to the question *'is it a feeling?'* is *'yes'*. If, however *'lover'* is to be guessed the correct answer to the same question is *'no'*. When forming the concept of *'love'* the characteristics we stress are the characteristics of a feeling (that is, of a characteristic). Similarly, we can say of snow that it is white, of white that it is a color, but if *'snow'* is to be found out, the answer to the question *'is it a color?'* will be *'no'*. We cannot affirm that snow is a color. That is, the characteristics of characteristics can not always be affirmed of the thing which has these characteristics.

'Cain's brother' is a concrete concept because it refers to a person in its relationship to another person. But *'brotherhood'*, *'kinship'* are abstract concepts because in these we think about the relations themselves and not about the persons who are thus related."

"I think this much theory was enough for me. Let's go on playing. I have a difficult question in mind."

"Not today. Maybe tomorrow. But until then I will tell you some examples which could be objects of Bar Kochba games. You have to decide what you would answer to the questions I spoke about today."

"Let me hear the concepts."

"I will tell you presently, but first I propose to review quickly what we have been talking about. What kinds of concepts do you remember?"

"There are individual concepts, general concepts, collective or not-collective concepts, and then concrete and abstract concepts. These are all I remember."

"What do you call concepts when no really existing object possesses the totality of characteristics that make up its contents?"

"Oh yes. They are empty concepts. I almost forgot this kind, although they are the most interesting ones."

"Now, let us consider one by one the questions you may ask when you inquire about the different kinds of concepts."

"'Is it a singular thing?' I ask this question when I want to know if the concept is individual or general. When the answer is 'yes', it is an individual concept, when it is 'no', it is a general concept.

'Is it an imaginary thing only?' When the answer is 'yes', the concept is empty. If it is an individual concept than I can ask whether it is a group of things about which we think as a single thing. If the answer is 'yes' than this is an individual collective concept. In the case of general collective concepts I can ask whether one of these things is a collection of different things.

"That's right. Later I wish to make your knowledge regarding empty concepts more exact.

Now, here is a list of Bar Kochba examples. Tell me, to what kinds of concepts they belong: 'World's first astronaut', 'universe', 'heroism', 'funker'.

Attention, please! I am 'Log Ice'. I kindly ask the reader to stop reading whenever I appear. First let the reader try to answer the questions or the problems!

Solutions to the problems:
The next day I heard Vera's answers to the problems posed on the previous day. She solved them correctly, as follows:

The 'Word's first astronaut' is an individual, concrete concept. It is not empty and not a collective concept.

'Universe' is an individual, concrete, non-empty and collective concept.

'Heroism' is a general, abstract, non-empty and not a collective concept.

'Funker' is a general, concrete, non-empty and not a collective concept.

Yes, no

'Living being', 'lifeless thing', 'concept' are such categories in Bar Kochba by which we divide possible things into three great groups. If the thing to be guessed belongs to one category, it belongs to none of the other two. 'Lifeless thing', 'living being', 'concept' are incompatible with one another.

Two concepts are **incompatible** when there is nothing that can belong to the extensions of both concepts. Thus, for example, 'peace' and 'war', 'copper' and 'iron', 'iron' and 'love' are incompatible pairs of concepts. On the contrary, concepts the extensions of which may include the same things, are **compatible**. For example, 'metal object' and 'iron object' are compatible because the extension of 'iron object' may include things which also belong to the extension of 'metal object'. This latter differs from the former in that its extension may also include copper objects, gold objects beside iron objects. These concepts have the **relationship of genus and species**. This is one case of compatibility. The concept of **genus** has a wider extension, the extension of the **species** concept is made up by parts of things belonging to the concept of genus. Things belonging to the concept of species have all the characteristics of the genus, and moreover, have other, so called species characteristics. All that we can say about things belonging to the concept of genus can be said of things belonging to its species concept, but these latter have some common characteristics which can not be found in other species belonging to the same genus. These are their specific characteristics, these differentiate them from other species within the genus.

"Now, let's begin playing."

"My first task is to establish to which category the thing belongs that I have to guess. Is it a living being?"

"Yes".

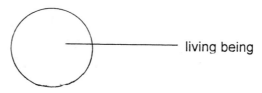

living being

"So it belongs to the category of living beings. Now I look for the species concept by narrowing down the extension of the category. Is it an animal?"

"Yes"

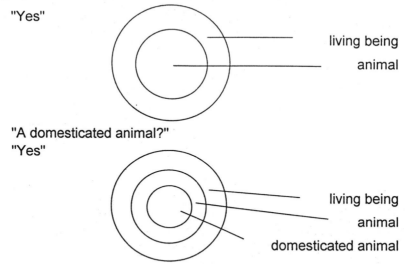

living being
animal

"A domesticated animal?"
"Yes"

living being
animal
domesticated animal

"The species concept of the category of 'living being' is 'animal'. I am lucky because I have always asked the species to which the thing to be guessed belongs. There are some species within a genus. When a thing within a genus belongs to one species, it can not belong to another species.

"That is, the species within a genus are also incompatible" says Vera. "Now, if you asked, 'is it a mammal?', I would say 'no'. What do you know from this?"

"The answer 'no' also gives information. From this I know that what I have to guess belongs to the extension of the negative concept, *'not-mammal'*. When we separate a species within the genus on the basis of some characteristics, we can generalize all the other things belonging to the concept of genus in a negative concept on the basis that they do not possess the given characteristics.

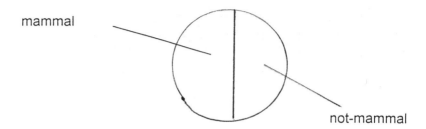

mammal

not-mammal

When I know what characteristics are lacking in something, I have got nearer to get to know it because I have excluded certain things from the inquiry. Now, I have to ask the species concepts of this concept."

"Please, wait a little! I think I have learned about what you are saying. It seems to be very similar to what I have learnt in mathematics. I have learned that if set *B* is a subset of set *A*, then there is a *non-B* set whose members are exactly the things that are members of *A* but not of *B*. We mark the *'non-B'* set like this: *-B*."

"That's correct. Now you have told it in the language of mathematics what I was speaking about. A set in logic appears as the extension of a concept. As I have told you, the extension of a concept is a class, and in this case the words 'class' and 'set' can be used as synonyms.
But let's go on. Now I have to ask the species concept of a *'not-mammal'*.
Is it a certain thing?"

"No."

"Now, I try to approach it from another direction. I choose another characteristic, and put the question accordingly.
Is it in the possession of somebody?

"Yes."

"What is the relation between the extension of the concepts *'not-mammal domesticated animal'* and *'thing which is in the possession of somebody?'*"

"Some but not all not-mammal domesticated animals which are in the possession of somebody. But among the things which are in the possession of somebody there can be domesticated not-mammal animals and things which are different from a domesticated not-mammal animal. Thus the extension of both concepts include things which also belong to the extension of the other one, but there are things which do not belong to the extension of the other concept."

thing in the possession of somebody

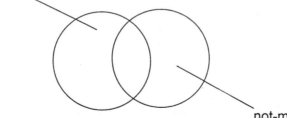

domesticated
not-mammal animal

"The relation between these concepts is called the relation of partial coincidence or that of intersection. These concepts are compatible because there are things which belong to the extension of both concepts. From the answer 'yes' we learn that in the given situation we have to guess such a thing which belongs to the extension of both concepts."

"Wait a little, something has just occurred to me. If the relationship between concepts A and B is that of partial coincidence then their extension together becomes the union of the *A* and *B* sets, which we mark in mathematics like this

$$A \cup B$$

The set A ∪ B is the **union** of the sets *A* and *B*. This set has as members everything that is either a member of *A* or of *B*.

You already know that the thing you are looking for is *'domesticated not-mammal animal'* and *'thing in the possession of somebody'*. To use the language of mathematics, you know that this thing is in the set the elements of which are the common and only the common elements of A and B. In mathematics we mark this set like this:

$$A \cap B$$

The set A ∩ B is the **intersection** of A and B. I.e. it is a set comprised of all elements that belong to both A and B."

"Excellent. But let us turn back to the concepts. A concept may, of course, intersect several concepts. Therefore I continue asking questions in order to delimit what I have to guess. The more concepts I ask which intersect the concept *'domesticated not-mammal animal'*, the more sides of the thing I get to know, which I have to guess."

I have learned from the answers that the thing in question can not be found in the universe of the real world, that it belongs to an imaginary world. It is a bird we do not usually think of as a bird; it weighs about 3 pounds and it belongs to somebody who has a farm.

Vera admitted, frankly, that she did not know the answer to some questions that I asked. It happens sometimes. There are so many questions that one can not be prepared to know the answer to each of the questions. From this I have learnt, however, that this community is not a big city in Hungary, because Vera knows the whereabouts of all the big cities in Hungary. There was a time during questioning when I thought I would never find the solution. But now I suspected what Vera had in mind. I wanted to ascertain if my guess was correct. I inquired about characteristics of which I thought they coincide with what I already knew, if my supposition was correct.

"May I heard it mentioned in a song?"

"Yes."

"Is this a song in which different animals are mentioned?"

"Yes."

"Does the farm belong to an old man?"

"Yes. Now, don't be afraid, tell me what is it?"

"Is it a chicken from old McDonald's farm?"

"Yes, it is!"

After a while Vera asked me whether 'yes' or 'no' are really sufficient for answering every questions.

"Each thing may or may not have a given characteristic, and therefore it is impossible that both a 'yes' and a 'no' answer could be correct. However, there may be some cases when the informant has some problems in answering the question. I do not think of a situation when the informant's knowledge is insufficient, yet he himself knows that the question is essential. Supposing I asked whether the color of the animal I have to guess is brown, what would you answer?"

"I don't know exactly. Because there are some brown and some white chicken. I think the correct answer is *not characteristic*."

"Yes. When several things, which belong to the extension of the general concept, have this characteristic and some others have not then the informant has to answer: 'not characteristic'."

"Yes, you have to guess the concept of genus, but the question refers to the characteristics of the species within the genus."

"That's so. But the correct answer is also *not characteristic* in case of an individual concept (which, as we know, has no species) when it has no importance whether the thing has or has not the characteristics respecting how the informant has this thing in mind. When the answer is *not characteristic* it means that it will not facilitate knowledge if the player learns that the thing which is to be guessed has the given characteristic or not. The *not characteristic* answer refers to the nature of a concept that it always reflects things only regarding some characteristics of it, while in forming the concept we disregard other characteristics.

The answer may cause a problem when the question is not definite enough or it has not been put quite exactly. This actually happens in Bar Kochba. *'What do you mean by...?'* is a question in which I call upon somebody to define the concept he uses. We will talk about it later."

"This talk has been very interesting. I like to see clearly the why of what I am doing even if it is only a game. But I should have to think it over again what that has got to do with the fact that I want to be a scholar."

"It is not difficult to see the connection. As I have said, a game is a simplified model of reality. In solving a scientific problem or any other task, we put questions to somebody or something from which we gain information. The informant can be other than a human being. Any object of cognition can give us information. This information, i.e.

the object of cognition, gives the 'yes' and 'no' information in its own fashion."

"I can quote an example. If a chemist wants to know the acid reaction of a solution, he dips a litmus paper into it. This is his informant. If the litmus paper turns red, it gives the answer 'yes' to the question whether the solution has acid reaction. If it turns blue, it answers that it has no acid reaction, that is, the solution is alkaline."

"This example is very good. But do you know what is the relation between the concepts *'acid reaction'* and *'non-acid reaction'*?"

"These concepts are incompatible."

"Yes, they are really incompatible. But incompatible concepts may have several relations. If the extension of two incompatible concepts make up the total extension of a genus concept, these two concepts have **contradictory relation** with each other. *'Acid reaction'* and *'non-acid reaction'* are contradictory concepts. But *'acid reaction'* and *'alkaline reaction'* are **co-ordinate** concepts because beside them we know *'neutrality'*, too. Therefore the concept *'non-acid reaction'* has a wider extension than the concept *'alkaline reaction'*."

"You are right, but not quite right. It depends on what you regard to be a genus concept."

"What do you have in mind?"

"If the genus concept is *'solution which changes the color of the litmus paper'*, this genus includes only acid solutions and alkaline solutions, therefore they are contradictory. Everything which is not acid, is alkaline. But if the genus concept is *'solution viewed from chemical effect'*, you are right."

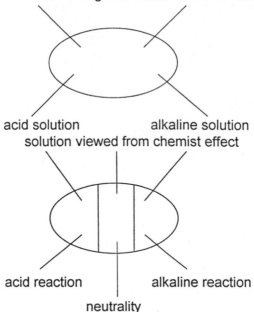

solution which changes the color of the litmus paper

acid solution   alkaline solution

solution viewed from chemist effect

acid reaction   alkaline reaction

neutrality

"Congratulations, this is really a clever idea! You have pointed out a very important aspect of correct thinking. We often make logical errors by not clarifying the extension of a negative concept. I will tell you an example:

Do you agree that if you have not lost something it is in your possession?"

"Yes, it is true."

"And is it true that you have not lost your horns?"

"Yes, it is."

"Now, I will make an inference from the two propositions:

What you have not lost is in your possession.
You have not lost your horns.
Therefore; You have horns."

"The inference seems to be logical. I will look into the mirror" said Vera smiling "if after all I have them."

She went to the mirror and was looking into it for a long time. I knew she was playing for time, and in the meantime she is thinking what was the error in the inference. Then she said:

"No, I have no horns."
"How is it possible?"

"I don't know. There must be some trouble with the concept 'not-lost thing'...
I have got it! The first proposition is true if I divide the genus *'things which have ever been in my possession'* into contradictory concepts: *'lost things'* and *'not-lost things'*. (But in this case the 'lost things' include worn out or destroyed things alike.) In the second proposition I have to choose a wider genus than the genus *'things which have ever been in my possession'*. My horn is a *'not-lost thing'*, which has never been in my possession. I have not lost it because I have never had it."

"The second proposition becomes true only in case the extension of the concept *'thing not lost'* includes not only the things you possess but also the things which you could not loose because you never possessed them, like your horns. Because the horns are not lost things, it does not follow that the horns are in your possession, that is, you have horns."

"It is good that you have reassured me about them. When did you figure out this - to be tactful - curious example?"

"It was not me, this was already used to the amusement of school-children in the Middle Ages."

"Will you give me other problems?"

"Yes, but first listen to me for a while. I wish to make solution of the problems easier for you by summing up the relationship of concepts."

"This will be fine."

```
            compatible                        incompatible
           /          \                      /            \
          /            \                    /              \
genus and species   intersection      contradictory    co-ordination
```

RELATION	CHARACTERIZATION
compatible	have common extension
genus and species	the extension of one (genus) includes the extension of the other concept (species)
intersection	the extensions of the two concepts have common parts, but there are things which belong only to the extension of one or the other
incompatible	their extensions have no common part; if something belongs to the extension of one it does not belong to the extension of the other
contradictory	the common extensions of the two concepts make up the extension of a genus
co-ordinate	two species of a genus whose common extension is smaller than the extension of the genus

"Now, I will give you your homework."

First problem: I give you pairs of concepts, you have to tell whether they are compatible. If yes, you have to decide whether the relationship is between genus and species, or is it intersection:

university student - American citizen
year - leap-year
high-school teacher - high-school student

Be careful when you solve the following problems:

year - month
county - district
hand - finger

The second problem is a funny story:

The students have to write a composition. They are impatient to know the results. John, Mike and Clara are all anxious to outdo one another, each of them would like to get better marks than the other.

The next morning they ask the teacher:

'Mr. Teacher, how did we do on the composition?'
'I can not tell you the marks, says the teacher.'
'But Mr. Teacher, do tell us something - plead the children.'
'Each composition included some good ideas, as well as some original ideas, but there were some mis-statements, too - says the teacher smiling under his mustache.'

The children are not very glad to hear this. They all know that they will not get the best mark from this strict teacher. But they expect equal marks. When they get back the compositions they are surprised to see that Mike got four, Clara a three and John mark a two. They ask the teacher how this was possible.

The teacher says:

'Mike's composition had some mis-statements. For this reason I could not give him mark 5. But all of his original ideas are good.
Some of Clara's original ideas are good but some of them are not.
John was not off the mark in everything. But none of his original ideas are good.'

This is the end of the story. Now you have to tell what the relationship is between the concepts *'good idea'* and *'original idea'*, if the genus is:
1.) *'idea in Mike's composition'*,
2.) *'idea in Clara's composition'*.
3.) *'idea in John's composition'*.

Solutions to the problem

"Did you find the pairs of concepts which are compatible?"

"Yes, I did. Only *'high-school teacher'* and *'high-school student'* are incompatible. *'University student'* and *'American citizen'* are intersections, *'year'* is the genus concept of *'leap-year'*."

"That's right. And how did you get on with the more difficult problems?"

"I was pondering over them for a long time. It was nice of you to call my attention to be careful, otherwise, I am afraid, I would have walked into the trap. After all I think that all three pairs of concepts are examples of incompatibility. First I thought that *'year'* is the genus concept for *'month'*, because a year consists of months, *'county'* is the genus concept for *'district'* because both are administrative units and the county consists of districts. *'Hand'* and *'finger'* seem to be intersections because there are toes and there are fingers."

"But is there a thing of which we can say that it is both a toe and a finger, similarly to a person who is both a university student and an American citizen?"

"No. It is precisely this which has led me to the correct solution. The hand ends in fingers. This is one of its characteristics. But we can not say this of a finger or of a toe. I can not say that *'there is a finger which ends in fingers'*. That is, the characteristics of a hand are not the characteristics of any of the fingers, therefore they are incompatible concepts."

Finger and hand bear the relationship of a part to the whole. The district is part of the county, month is part of the year. The characteristics of the whole are not always the same as the characteristics of the part. Therefore we can not be certain that what can be told of the whole, can also be told of the part. One who reasons that *'month'* is the species concept of *'year'* reasons erroneously, because he does not distinguish between the relationship of genus to species and the relationship of the part to the whole.

"How did you solve the other problem?"

"Within the genus *'idea in Mike's composition'* the species is *'good idea'*, and the species of this *'good idea'* is *'original idea'*.

Within the genus *'idea in Clara's composition'*, *'good idea'* and *'original idea'* are co-ordinate concepts.

What do you mean by ... ?

"I have promised you that we will talk about definition" I said to Vera one day.

"What do you mean by *'definition'*?"

"Just now you have asked me for the definition of *'definition'*. Namely, when we are asked *'What do you mean by..?'*, we usually answer with a definition.

"And did you just now give me the definition of *'definition'*?"

"No, I did not, since I haven't given you the characteristics by which you can differentiate it from anything else. *'Definition'* may be defined as follows: **Definition** is a logical operation the object of which is the exposition of the content of a concept.

"But if one does not know the meaning of *'content of a concept'*, one does not understand what you have said."

"That is true. This is why one of the usual requirements is that in definitions known concepts must be used. But this is more a pedagogical than a logical requirement. My definition was formally correct."

"Your definition might have been correct formally, but even though I know that the content of a concept is the totality of characteristics by which the things generalized within the concept may be differentiated from all other things, I do not learn much about definition by knowing that it is the exposition of the content of a concept."

"The role of definition in cognition is not to replace the exposition, the detailed explication. For instance when I say *'a triangle is a plane figure enclosed by three straight lines'*, I have given the definition of the triangle, but this by itself does not reveal many of the very important properties of the triangle.

We often use definitions for the purpose of clarifying what it is we wish to discuss, to ponder over.

The terms of everyday language in the expression of concepts are usually used without the need for preceding definition. When, for instance, I say, *'Yesterday I bought a new table for my room'*, you will of course not ask me, *'what do you mean by table?'*."

"I will not, because I know the meaning of the word 'table', that s, I know what it designates."

"You better not ask me the definition of 'table', because I would ɔe in trouble. I would be hard put to tell you the peculiar properties the thing we generalize in the concept of 'table' must possess."

"'Triangle' is a far more abstract something than 'table', yet it is ɛasier to define."

"Yes, this is so, because the meanings of terms belonging to the field of science are much more unequivocal than the terms used in everyday language. We seldom have to resort to definitions in everyday life. Usually only when we argue over something, and in the course of the argument it turns out that the difference of opinions is due to not having defined the contents of certain concepts."

"I have witnessed such an argument the other day. John and David were arguing over the existence of true love. According to John, such a thing does not exist, because true love should last for a lifetime, and in reality this is never so. David doubted this. He knew a couple who had started their relationship at a very young age, and were still in love when they were quite old.

> 'How can and old person be in love?' - asked John. 'Love is a flaming, intensified sexual desire. And this is a characteristic of the young only.'
> 'In my opinion' - said David - 'the essence of true love is the feeling of togetherness. The desire to be with the person I am in love with, to share our thoughts, to participate in the solving of our problems. In my opinion this is true love, and this feeling will not diminish with age, rather it might increase.
> This is how John answered:
> 'What are we really arguing about? If this is what you mean by true love, then you are right, it could last for a lifetime. But you mean something else by love than I do.'"

"He was right. He might have put it this way: your concept of love is different from mine. What they needed was to define what is the subject matter of their discuss. In other words they needed a definition of 'love'."

"I don't think this can be defined. Or is it logic that is able to define this feeling?"

"No, logic can not do that. It can only supply the guiding principles for what a correct definition ought to be, and it can tell you what typical mistakes are associated with definitions."

"It just occurs to me that I have recently read about such a mistake. I did not even understand what it was all about. I wanted to ask you, but I forgot.

Where did I read it?

Oh, now I remember! In Frigyes Karinthy's *Headings for the Big Encyclopedia*. Right at the beginning, under the heading *Interesting*.

Here is the book, I will read it to you:"

> *'What do we mean by it, why do we say it? What do we find interesting?'... He continues: 'How should I justify devoting a separate chapter to it. I feel that I can engage the readers interest only by assuring him that the word 'interesting' is a very interesting word, and it is worth analyzing. Of course, I must be extra careful not to commit the most obvious mistake of logical argument: not to mix the concept to be defined in with the defining concepts.'*

"Karinthy is referring here to the mistake of circular definition. But in order to understand this you must first get acquainted with the structure of definition.

A definition, as it appears from Karinthy's text as well, is composed of two parts: the definiendum and the definiens. The **definiendum** is the concept the content of which we wish to explain. In the **definiens** we enumerate the specificities that, taken together, are suited to distinguish the definiendum from all other things. I have already mentioned the definition of the triangle. In this definition *'triangle'* is the definiendum and *'plane figure enclosed by three straight lines'* is the definiens.

The definiens usually contains a concept that is broader than the definiendum, it contains one of the genera of the definiendum. In addition, the definiens indicates the characteristics of the species that distinguish the definiendum from other species within the genus. The genus in the definition of the triangle is *'plane figure'*.

We supply the characteristics of the species by pointing out that it is such a plane figure which is enclosed by three straight lines. Thus we

34

distinguish the triangle from other species of the genus, for instance from the quadrangle, which is enclosed by four straight lines.
Let's do a test to see if you have understood what I have told you:

> *'When we pronounce certain sounds, the flow of air is restricted by certain obstacles in our mouth. We call these sounds consonants.'*

Which concept here is the definiendum?"

"The definiendum is *'consonant'*."
"Within the definiens, which one is the genus and what characteristics of the species have I mentioned?"

"The genus is: *'sound'* and the characteristics of the species is: *'sound that is generated when the air-flow through our mouth encounters obstacles within our mouth'*."
"Well put.
The main rule of definition is that the definiendum and the definiens should be of equal extent. There are two mistakes possible in this respect.
The definition is too narrow, when the definiens enumerates characteristics that do not belong to all things that come under the definiendum.
The following definition is, for instance, too narrow:

> *'A planet is a celestial body circling the Sun, without it's own source of light.'*

This definition is too narrow because some other stars beside the Sun have planets.

The definition is too broad when all of the defining characteristics of the definiens also belongs to other things beyond the domain of the definiendum:

An example:

> According to a famous story it happens in the Academy at Athens in ancient times that somebody defined 'man' by 'featherless biped'. Hearing this, Diogenes, the philosopher, plucked a chicken and threw it over the wall into the Academy. He said: 'here was a featherless biped, surely, but just as surely it was not a man'."

"I see, the definiens was too broad. That's clear, but I want to ask you something else. You say that the definition of a planet as *'celestial body circling around the Sun and lacking it's own light source'* is incorrect because it is too narrow. But why could we not mean just such a thing under *'planet'*? Who can prevent me from using the term *'planet'* in this sense?"

"No one. And if before starting a dialogue about something, you make known the sense which you will give to that thing, in other words, you define it, then you can define it any way you wish. This is what happens when a new word is introduced into a language, usually into the language of a science. Such a definition is called a **nominal definition**.

We can accept as a nominal definition, for instance, what Humpty Dumpty said to Alice in `Through the Looking-Glass...` when she asked what was an un-birthday present: *'A present given when it isn't your birthday'*."

"And if I give it a nominal definition, I can introduce any new word into a language?"

"What are you thinking of?"

"I am thinking that for instance, from now I will call brushes and dogs by the common word 'brogs'."

"You may do that, but don't except the word 'brogs' to be generally accepted as part of everyday language. Only words that are useful for the purpose of social interaction will become part of the vocabulary of a language. It is useless to give a nominal definition if nobody needs it, if it is contrived, and serves no useful purpose.

The majority of words in the common language did not become part of the language by being introduced through nominal definition. The words of the common language obtained more or less definite meaning in the course of communication between people. It should be remembered that human interaction would become extremely complicated, perhaps even impossible, if all the words used had to be defined first. Therefore, if we want to be understood, we must use words that have conceptual contents developed in the course of usage.

But to use words with conceptual contents different from the usual, without first defining them, is absolutely not permissible. It is a grave logical mistake because in this way the words do not obey, do not fulfill the function of communicating our thought to others.

Listen, I will read to you a relevant passage from *'Through the Looking-Glass'*:

> *'I don't know what you mean by 'glory',' Alice said.*
> *Humpty Dumpty smiled contemptuously. 'Of course you don't - till I tell you. I meant 'there's a nice knock-down argument for you!'*
> *'But 'glory' doesn't mean 'a nice knock-down argument', Alice objected.*
> *'When I use a word', Humpty Dumpty said, in rather a scornful tone, 'it means just what I choose it to mean - neither more nor less.'*
> *'The question is'. said Alice, 'whether you can make words mean so many different things.'*
> *'The question is', said Humpty Dumpty, 'who is to be master - that's all.'*

What do you think of Humpty Dumpty?"

"I think he was a pompous eggheaded ass!"

"Come now, why all the heat?"

"I have suddenly become so angry at him because I remembered some such Humpty Dumpty characters among my acquaintances. Just imagine, the other day we were arguing with David over some matter, and when it turned out, in the course of discussion, that he was wrong, he simply declared: 'You can not understand me because you can not conceive of the meaning of the words the way I use them. It is way beyond your understanding'. At other times he uses expressions we have never heard before. David is like Humpty Dumpty, he believes that 'he is master, and that's all'".

"Yes, unfortunately there are many such Humpty Dumpties. We'd do better avoiding them. The best way to deal with them is to ask them, as frequently as we can: What do you mean by..?"

"If I should ask you 'what do you mean by having definite form?', is it certain that you will answer with a definition?"

"No, it is not at all certain. But why did you think of this question?"

"I was just working on a crossword puzzle when we started our conversation, and I can not think of the answer to 24 Down, which is 'Having a definite form'. What does this mean?"

"I don't know it either. But I have an idea. Let us end our conversation, and continue after you have solved the entire puzzle."

"Did I offend you by changing the subject?"

"Not at all. I want to use the crossword puzzle for giving you an assignment. In solving a crossword puzzle you are performing logical operations. You are looking for definiendum to fit the definiens, for genus to fit species and vice versa, etc. What I want you to do is to identify the instances where the definiens was given and you had to find the definiendum. For instance, if 17 Across would be *'A chess piece that can move and capture in a straight direction'*, the answer would be *'rook'*. *'Rook'* is the definiendum; the definiens whatever is given in the information.

'I see. And if the given information would be *'chess piece'*, and the answer *'rook'*, then one of the species would have to be guessed on the basis of the genus."

"And this is just what I wanted to continue my talk with. But I can see that you already understand your second assignment: look for examples of relationships between concepts in the crossword puzzle. In other words: select the instances where you are able to ascertain the nature of the conceptual relationship between information and solution. General names, - as I have told you before - are usually the linguistic expressions of concepts, so my advice to you is: find general names in the information or the solution and ignore the other expressions like proper names, verbs, etc."

Vera took a newspaper and began to work the crossword puzzle. When she finished she said:

"I have found quite a few definitions in the crossword puzzle. But there might be even more than I have noticed. In some instances I could not decide weather or not I could regard them as definitions. For example, I am not certain that when only one word is given, such as for example 'broadcasting' it can be considered as definition."

"What were the solutions associated with this item of information in the crossword?"

"'Broadcasting' is 'airing'. I think their extensions are equal. That is why I believe that it is a correct definition in this respect."

"This is not the problem. The problem is that this word-pair is not the linguistic expression of different concepts. In my opinion we are merely replacing a word with another word that has the same meaning. Some people consider this act as definition. They are right to the extend that whoever knows one of the two words, but does not know the other one, will acquire new knowledge by this act. This kind of definition is called **verbal definition**, that is an act revealing the meaning of a certain word."

"I have found genus and species relationships between some of the pairs. The *'airplane type'* is the genus of *'jumbo'*, the *'word of denial'* is the genus of *'no'*. Because there are several radio programs in the subject of transportation, *'on the road'* is the species of *'programs dealing with transportation'*, and finally, the species of the concept of *'noble beverage'* is *'ancient vintage'* because *'champagne'* is also a *'noble beverage'*."

"Very good!"

"I have found an example for intersection. *'Ulcer'* is a *'stomach ailment'*, but it can be other than *'stomach ailment'* as well, and there exist other *'stomach ailments'* than *'ulcer'*.

By the way, I heard that stomach ulcers can be caused by nervous stress as well."

"True. But what does that have to do with this?"

"It has to do with the fact that this crossword puzzle analysis is beginning to get on my nerves. Let's put an end to it."

"Very well. See you later!"

The Chest-problem

"Imagine a very large chest into which we can put all things of the word!"

"It is impossible because the world is infinite, it contains an infinite number of things, therefore we can not put them into a chest."

"And if the chest is infinitely big?"

"Even so there is a problem. This chest too belongs to the contents of the world, so this chest should also be put into the chest which is evidently impossible."

"All right, we do not really need this infinitely large chest. We shall consider as the contents of the world that we want to put into the chest only the things that can serve as objects of a given inquiry. It is this narrow world that we call the **universe of discourse**. (The word 'universe' derives from the Latin, it means the 'world' or 'cosmos', the totality of all things.)

For our purposes the meaning of 'universe' is restricted to whatever can be taken into consideration for our inquiry. Scholars also follow the same course. For them the universe of discourse may be the world of living things, the world of physical phenomena that take place in the process of thinking, etc.. Scholarly investigation always takes place within a more or less precisely circumscribed 'world'. Such a universe of discourse may also consist of an infinite number of things but at least it has the advantage that it does not present an unsolvable problem such as putting a chest into a chest.

When we limit our inquiry to a universe of discourse, we recognize that we can not have any single concept by which we can reflect everything. All the more so because we can form concepts about our concepts of things. Sometimes the subject of our thinking, - that is the thing what we are thinking about, - is the world of our concepts."

"I think, just now we are also thinking and talking about our concepts. For example, when you told that there were individual concepts then you were talking about the world of concepts."

"What would be your answer to the question whether the 'individual concept' is an individual concept or not?"

The 'individual concept' is a general concept because there is more then one individual concept. For example, the *'first dog who traveled to space'*, or *'my favorite cookie'* are individual concepts and they belong to the extension of the 'individual concept'."

"But an individual concept is a concept what we defined as a concept to the extension of which belongs only one thing. How is it possible, then, that into the extension of 'individual concepts' belongs not only one thing?"

"Oh, I think, this problem is similar to the riddle:

May the company barber shave himself when he is ordered to shave only those who can not shave themselves. Those, however, who can, must shave themselves. So the barber violates the order if he shaves, because he may shave only those who can not shave themselves; but if he does not shave, he also violates the order, because all who can shave themselves must do so."

"Yes, this is the same as the problem of the chest. Therefore we should know that no concept can be a concept of itself. No concept can be ranged with the things belonging to the domain of concepts whose domain consists of the given things."

"Why is this important for me to know?"

"Because this is the point where the logical error which we call the exchange of concepts is often committed. People disregard the fact that a concept is always determined within a given universe of discourse, and when we change the universe of discourse, all previously given definitions may lose their validity."

"How do you mean this?"

"First I will tell you an example from Bar Kochba. What would be your comment if somebody told you that *'Cupid's arrow'* is not an empty concept because in Greek mythology Cupid does have an arrow?"

"I see, you want to say that *'Cupid's arrow'* is an empty concept when the universe of discourse is the world of material objects, but it is not empty when the universe of discourse includes concepts because we have such a concept.

In your list which you told me earlier *'Desdemona's handkerchief'* is featured within the given universe of discourse: *'In Shakespeare's Othello'*. Then it can not be regarded here as an empty concept?"

"I do not think that this serves to provide the universe of discourse. Because - when *'Desdemona's handkerchief'* is to be found out -, the informant of the Bar Kochba would say *'no'* to the question whether we speak about an existing thing, although Desdemona's handkerchief exists in the universe of *'things mentioned in Shakespeare's works'*. By contrast, for example the concept of *'Desdemona's discotheque costume'* will be empty in this universe of discourse."

"Can we also ask such a question in Bar Kochba?"

"Why not, and if the contestant makes it clear that all the *'things invented by the informant'* belong to the universe of discourse, he or she may even hope to find the solution."

"I will always clarify the universe of discourse whenever I play."

"You better keep this in mind even when you are not playing. When you want to deal with languages you will see how often this problem arises, for example, in translating from one language into another."

"Will you give me an example?"

"Gladly. Tell me, what is wrong with the following reasoning:

The mouse likes cheese.
The word mouse consists of five letters.
Therefore;   there is something which consists of five letters and likes cheese.

"The trouble is that in the first sentence the universe of discourse consists of living beings while in the second proposition it consists of words. Therefore the two occurrences of the word *'mouse'* are the verbal expressions of two different concepts."

"That's right. I have taken this example from a Latin grammar-book. Mouse is *'mus'* in Latin. The word *'mus'* consists of three letters. Therefore the servile translation should have been:

The mouse likes cheese.
The word mouse consist of three letters.
Therefore;   *there is something which consists of three letters and likes cheese.*

"But then I would have disregarded the fact that I have to change over from the universe of discourse of Latin words to the universe of discourse of English words. When I want to translate something correctly which is valid in the universe of one language, I have to find that which corresponds to it in the universe of discourse of the other language, and this is not always simple.

Every scientific statement represents a truth within some universe of discourse. This, however, has become clear only in the light of the scientific results of the past two centuries. Earlier it seemed there were scientific truths that represented eternal unconditional truths. The tenets of Euclidean geometry, for example, were regarded as such."

"But you do not want to say that what we learn in geometry is not always true?"

"This is not the case. These tenets are always true under given conditions, that is, in the given universe of discourse, in plane geometry. But if we change the universe of discourse, the conditions cease to exist that permit the validity of certain laws of geometry. You have learned, for example, that the sum of the angles of the triangle equals 180 degrees. This is always true when you start out from the axioms of Euclidean geometry. Nobody has denied that these characteristics of the triangle can be derived from the axioms of Euclidean geometry. But at the beginning of the past century other geometries were constructed. For example, Lobachevski, managed to build an intrinsically consistent geometrical system which replaced one of the axioms of Euclidean geometry, namely the axiom of

43

parallelism, by its negation. In Lobachevski's geometrical system the sum of the angles of the triangle equals less than 180 degree. The basic difference between the two geometrical systems is that while in Euclidean geometry the universe is plane, in Lobachevski's geometry it is saddle-shape. Look, I will draw it for you:

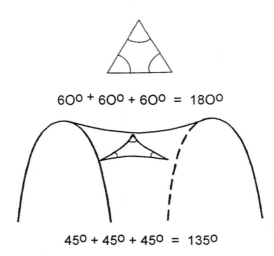

$$60^o + 60^o + 60^o = 180^o$$

$$45^o + 45^o + 45^o = 135^o$$

The point is, it was proven: the tenets of Euclidean geometry are not unconditionally true as it was believed earlier. It was proven that some conditions can be changed and in this new system old definitions lose their validity."

"I am afraid I do not understand everything you have said. But I understand that the definition we have learned is the definition of the *'triangle'* in plane geometry. The meaning of the word *'triangle'* is different in Lobachevski's geometry."

"It is enough for now if you have understood this much, because we have only spoken about the importance of defining the universe of discourse."

Putting the things into boxes

"Let's set things right in the chest!"

"How can we do it?"

"We will divide the things in the chest into groups according to their characteristics."

"Let's begin! Let us choose one characteristic and let's simply call it characteristic A. Of this A we know only that it is one of the different characteristics the things in the chest may possess, but it is not certain that they posses it."

We divide the chest into two parts. To the right we place those things that possess characteristic A,- we will call them A things - and we put the other things to the left, namely those things about which we can not tell that they have characteristic A. We will call them *non-A* things. I will draw the chest:

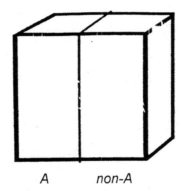

A   *non-A*

Thus, the first step of putting things into a box has taken place. Although there are some problems. Sometimes it is difficult to decide on which side certain things belong. Even a simple characteristic like *'red thing'* may pose a problem.

"Where should we put the red-spotted ball?"

We decide to put only those things among the red ones that are only red. As this ball is of various colors, we will put it among the non-red things.

"Could we decide otherwise?"

"Yes. The point is that we have to know what we are doing and why we are doing it. First we have to decide on the point of view on the basis of which we reach a decision, and then we have to stick to it. In reality there is no clear-cut demarcation line between the properties of things. But if we wish to think about them, we always have to 'put them into boxes'."

"I do not like putting things into boxes! Is it not what they call dogmatic, rigid thinking?"

"No, it is not. What we are doing now is the necessary condition for logical thinking. When you say that the ball has the characteristic of being red, and you put it among the red things, and then you say that it does not have this characteristic and take it out of there, it will not take you far. You will have to decide somehow! The person who is not willing to acknowledge that decision-making is a complicated matter, and never wants to change his or her decision, is thinking rigidly and dogmatically. Why should we not regroup the things in the chest when we think it useful? We can regroup them, although we have to know why we do it, and we have to be careful to put everything in order again!"

"What if we divide the chest into three parts? This way we could put the red things into one part, the not-red things into the other part, and those that represent a border-line between red and not-red things into the third one. I would put here, for example, those things that are almost pink or have a little red on them."

"You can do it, but your task will not have become easier. Again, it will be difficult to decide what you regard to be almost pink, and how much red means *a little red*. You have to draw the lines yourself, and these will be more or less artificial. Drawing these more or less artificial lines is the precondition that makes you able to think about things and about the fact that **in reality there are no sharp border-lines between things.**"

"That's true. But let's go on getting things right!"

"Let's put a shelf into the chest in horizontal position. Let us put *B* things, that is things which have characteristic *B*, on the upper shelf, and the *non-B* things, that do not have characteristic *B*, on the lower shelf. In this way we will have four 'boxes' in the chest.

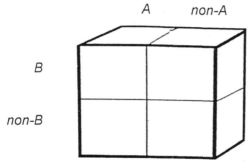

A   non-A

B

non-B

From now I will represent our imaginary chest in this way:

1.	3.
2.	4.

I have numbered the boxes. Each number is the name of a box."

"This reminds me when I was a little child and was in a hospital for having my tonsils removed, there were four of us in a room. And the nurse called us *'Number One'*, *'Number Two'*."

"Yes, she knew very little about you and called you according to the bed in which you were lying."

"Later, as Eve was always crying, she was called *'Crybaby'*. Clara once asked, *'Who is the Crybaby?'* It is *'Number Three'* - we said because we knew that Eve was called by both names."

"How could we call the things in the various boxes another way?"

"We could call a thing in box 1 *'A'* and we can call it *'B'* too."

"That's right, because the things in box 1 have property *A* and have property *B*, but they are the only things that have both *A* and *B* properties. Therefore, *'thing in box 1'* and *'thing which has properties*

A and B' (or for short, *A and B*) denote the same thing, but on the basis of different properties. Things which have properties *A* and *non-B* belong in box 2, things which have *non-A* and *B* properties belong in box 3, and at last, things which have *non-A* and *non-B* properties belong in box 4."

1. *A* *B*	3. *non-A* *B*
2. *A* *non-B*	4. *non-A* *non-B*

I hope you see there may be a case when we cannot find things in every box."

"That is, it is possible that some of the boxes are empty."

"Right.

Will you tell me, please, what is the relation between the concept of *'thing which has A property'* and the concept of *'thing which has B property'* if you can find something only in boxes 1 and 4?"

"It is a difficult question."

"Well, I will help you. Let's take the following concepts:

a/ *'living being with soft ear-lobe'*, and

b/ *'living being which is able to make instruments of production'*.

Excuse me for the strange idea, but if we placed all living beings into a big chest and then we would arrange them on basis whether they have soft ear-lobe or not (*A, non-A*) and on the basis whether they are able to make instruments of production or not (*B, non-B*), we would notice that all human beings would be crowded in box 1, because human beings have soft ear-lobe and are able to make instruments of production. Therefore *'living being with soft ear-lobe'* and *'living being which is able to make instruments of production'* are concepts that have the same extension. The two concepts differ from one another as regards their content; that is, we have the same thing in mind, but on the basis of different characteristics. We call these concepts equivalent concepts."

"But where could we find the other living beings?'

"They all would be crowded in box 4.
By the way, I would like to ask you something. Can the player of Bar Kochba find the answer to the informant's notion when he thought of an equivalent concept as a solution?"

"I think this can not be accepted as a right solution. This would contradict the idea that the player's task is to find out the thing that we have thought of in the form of a concept.

"I also think so! **Equivalent concepts** are different concepts. The knowledge of one of them does not imply the knowledge of the other one. Thus, for example, if John knows that people and only people are those living beings who are capable of making instruments of production, it does not imply that John also knows that people and only people belong to the living beings who have soft earlobes. It is the same as when your friend Clara knew who 'Number Three' was, but did not know who 'Crybaby' was, although Eve was called by both names.
But let us turn back to our chest. If I open box 1 and I see that it is not empty, what can you state about things A in relation to things B?

"I can state that there are some A things which are B things."

"Yes, or a shorter version: 'Some A are B'. Let us suppose that objects that have property A are things that are egg-shaped and the objects that have property B are red. In this case what can you tell about the relation of A to B?"

"There are egg-shaped things that are red, or I can tell: 'Some egg-shaped thing is red'. Are these statements synonyms?"

"We shall use these two types of statements as synonyms, as different linguistic expressions of the same relation.
Now, another question to you:
Please, tell me do you also know that there are objects that are egg-shaped and are not red?"

"Precisely what are you asking? I know that there are objects which are egg-shaped and are not red, such as for example footballs, but I know this not from the fact that we looked into box 1 and stated that it was not empty."

"That is a clever answer. What you have said can also be formulated this way: If the proposition *'There are some A that are B'* is true; it does not imply that the proposition *'There are some A that are non-B'* is also true. Henceforward be careful to distinguish between knowledge you have acquired trough logical reasoning and knowledge you otherwise have."

"Can I acquire new knowledge about *A* through logic if I know that *'There are some A which are B'*?"

"Yes, you can. For example, that *'There are some A that do not belong to non-B'*, or to put it more briefly, *'There are some A that are not non-B'*. From this you will know that you cannot find all *A* objects in the *non-B* box. This, of course, does not exclude the possibility that there do not exist *A* things that are *non-B* things
But let me ask you further questions and, please wait with yours. First I would like you to learn about some kinds of simple propositions as I wish to talk to you about inferences drawn from these propositions."

"All right, but please, open your imaginary boxes quickly. And please, do not ask me what I should say about *A* if there is something in the box, and then what I should say about *B*, and what I should say about *non-A* and *non-B*; all that is so boring. The matter is very simple. I know what kind of things can be in boxes 1, 2, 3, and 4. If there is at least one thing in the box, I can say that such a thing exists."

"Well, all right. Is it also clear what you are going to say of A if box 2 is empty?

"Yes. If box 2 is empty I say 'No A are non-B'."

"That's right. But, tell me please, where is a thing A - if it is exist at all - when it is true that 'No A are non-B'?"

"In this case every A is B, that means every A is in the box 1, where the B things are."

"Yes. Subsequently we shall interpret the proposition 'Every A is B' and the proposition 'All A are B' - which we interpret as similar to 'Every A is B' - as abbreviations, or if you like, simplified linguistic expressions of the proposition 'No A are non-B'".

"Don't you get annoyed if I interrupt you?"

"Of course not. I am glad to hear any question, but sometimes I am afraid we shall digress from the subject and it will be more difficult for you to follow what I am going to say, but always ask when you have a question."

"Could we interpret the statement 'All A are B' in any other way than 'No A are non-B'?"

"Yes, because in everyday language the statements 'All A are B' and 'Every A is B' are used in several senses. For example, let us suppose that I say 'All apples in my bag are red apples'. But what will you say if you look into my bag and find no apple there?"

"I will say that you have cheated me because there is no apple in your bag."

"Yes, you would say this because you have supposed that there are apples in my bag. That is, in this case you have interpreted the statement *'All apples in my bag are red'* (that is the proposition which has the form *'All A are B'*) as a compound proposition. Its components are: *'There are apples in my bag'* (*'A exists'*) and *'No apples in my bag are not red'* (*'No A are non-B'*).

Now, let us take another example: The leader of a course tells the students at the first class that *'All students who skip a class have to account for their absence'*. Certainly, this proposition does not include such a proposition that *'there is a student who skips a class'*. So, this is another interpretation of the proposition *'All A are B'*"

"Then which is the correct interpretation of the proposition *'All A are B'*?"

"There is no such thing as the only correct interpretation. You know that one and the same statement in everyday language may have various meanings. It is the task of logic to point out such ambiguities and to call attention to the possibility of logical errors that follow from ambiguity. One who knows about ambiguity can avoid making errors. But sometimes we use such an ambiguity on purpose. Listen to the following story:

> *Robert is happy to tell his father who has just arrived home that he has completed the home work he was given that morning. Claudia, his sister, interrupts him: 'Robert is not telling the truth: he has just told me that he's got no homework for today'.*

What is your opinion, could Robert have told the truth both to his sister and father?

"If he wanted to say that there is no homework that he was given that morning and did not complete, he told the truth. Anyway, in my opinion this Robert is a cunning boy. He wanted to make use of the fact that his father received no training in logic and does not know the possibility of misunderstanding that comes from the different interpretation of *'All A are B'*."

"Well, not like *'some'* who have learned logic, since we have much less chance to mislead them. Let me hear then how these people solved the problem of categorical propositions."

"I do not know what you are talking about. What do you mean by the categorical proposition? There has been no mention of them!"

"Oh, you are right! I have to wait to give you some homework till I explain what I mean by categorical proposition."

Categorical propositions

"The propositions about which we have spoken are generally called categorical propositions. In my opinion, the basic forms are the following:"

> *Some A are B*
> *Some A are non-B*
> *All A are B*
> *No A are B*

"Why do you say that *'are generally called'*, and *'in my opinion'*? Why the vagueness?"

"You ask difficult questions. But, since you ask, I shall try to make clear what the problem is.

It was Aristotle, who lived from 384 to 322 B. C., who worked out the first theory of categorical propositions and the correct inferences that can be drawn from them. He, however, formulated it in accordance with the structure of old Greek language. For example, instead of saying *'All A are B'* and *'Some A are non-B'*, he expressed them in a more properly translated form: *'B belongs to all A'* and *'B does not belong to some A'*. But he used other linguistic variants as well. Now it is not very simple to decide whether the various linguistic expressions are only different linguistic variants or whether they also differ from one another from a logical point of view. It has some basis when we suppose that certain translations - by which Aristotelian logic was rendered into contemporary, everyday language, or in the language of recently established logical systems - have brought about essential changes as regards the original thoughts.

The propositions which I called categorical propositions are only similar to those we can find in Aristotelian logic and differ from them in several points."

"In what points do they differ, for example?"

"For example, I call those forms basic forms when I state something about *A* things in relation to *B* or *non-B* things. We can deduce such propositions from them which we infer from the relationship of *A* with *B* to its relationship with *non-B*. Furthermore, we can deduce propositions from them that express the relationship of *B* or *non-B* to *A* and/or *non-A*. In the meantime I regard the proposition *'Some A is non-B'* only as a linguistic variant of the proposition *'B does not belong to some A'*, while Aristotle distinguished them logically. For him these two meanings are not mutual consequences of each other, but in a number of subsequent logical systems the differences are left out of consideration."

"Oh, this is very complicated!"

"You see, it was for a good reason that I was afraid to be involved in this problem. I have to say, again, that it would be of no use to think that only one correct interpretation can be given of propositions of Aristotle's logic."

"That is, it must be what it would seem to be. Do you know why I say this? Because these complicated things remind me of a passage in *Alice's Adventures in Wonderland*. I have to read it to you. Listen please, with both ears. The Duchess says:

> *'Be what you would seem to be'* - or if you'd like it put more simply - *'Never imagine yourself not to be otherwise than what it might appear to others that what you were or might have been was not otherwise than what you had been would have appeared to them to otherwise.'*
> *'I think I should understand it better'*, Alice said very politely, *'if I had it written down; but I can't quite follow it as you say it.'*"

"I have understood your example. In fact, sometimes it will be easier to understand an idea if we write down. Sometimes even formulae are more understandable than inscriptions in everyday language. Therefore I will write down the formulae of some categorical propositions which can be deduced from basic forms. I suppose you already know that deducibility means that if that from which I deduce something is true, that conclusion is also true.

BASIC FORM	THE FORM DEDUCED FROM THE BASIC FORM
Some A are B	*Some B are A* *Some A are not non-B* *Some B are not non-A*
Some A are non-B	*Some non-B are A* *Some A are not B* *Some non-B are not non-A*
No A are B	*No B are A* *All A are non-B* *All B are non-A*
All A are B	*No A are non-B* *No non-B are A* *All non-B are non-A*

"Maybe you get frightened by these formulae, but now I quote the Duchess:

'That's nothing to what I could say if I chose.'"

"Oh, that's enough! I don't want to know any more about it. It's already getting difficult for me to follow."

"All right ... I just wanted to ask whether in your opinion the proposition *'No non-B are A'* follows from *'All A are B'*, in the case where both propositions affirm the existence of the things (*A*, *B*) we are speaking about."

"Do you have in mind what we have said about the apple and Robert's lesson?"

"Yes."

"Well, let us see. In this case the proposition *'All A are B'* affirms that *A* exists and *B* exists and the proposition *'No non-B are A'* ... now, in this case whose existence do we suppose?"

"Just think a bit, of what objects do we affirm something? Of *non-B* objects?"

"Yes, here we suppose that there are *non-B*. But this supposition does not occur in the first proposition. that is, in this case the proposition *'No non-B are A'* does not follow from *'All A are B'*."

"And now tell me whether the proposition *'Some A are B'* follows from *'All A are B'* if we suppose the existence of A and B things."

"Yes, it does; it's only natural. If *'All A are B'* and we suppose that A exists, we can say that *'There are A which are B'*, i. e. *'Some A are B'*."

"If, however *'All A are B'* is a kind of proposition in which we do not suppose the existence of A, it will not follow from it that *'There are A which are B'*. But if we suppose that A, B, and even *non-A* and *non-B* exist, then all of our inferences that we have talked about will be valid."

"Oh, stop there! That is quite enough! You are just like our mathematics teacher. He is very clever man who knows a lot and wants to explain everything to us. His usual phrase is *'Now, I will put it more precisely'*. But he does not realize that we cannot follow him, and everything gets confused, just like right now."

"All right! But don't be angry with me. Let us agree that subsequently we will use only those deduced forms that have been written down for you in the schedule, and from among the four basic forms in which we suppose that only in the propositions *'Some A are B'* and *'Some A are non-B'* do we suppose the existence of objects that we speak of in the proposition. I will make your task even easier by drawing our chest again, and I will mark with an asterisk the box, about which you know, on the basis of the basic form, that it contains something. If you know from the basic form that a box is empty, I will mark it with an 0.

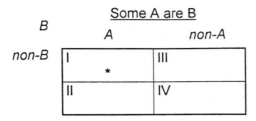

Some A are B

B
	A	non-A
non-B	I *	III
	II	IV

Some A are non-B

B
	A	non-A
non-B	I	III
	II *	IV

No A are B

B
	A	non-A
non-B	I O	III
	II	IV

All A are B

B
	A	non-A
non-B	I	III
	II O	IV

If you look at these drawings it becomes clear that the forms we have deduced from the basic forms are such that their truth follows from the truth of the basic form."

"Well, I am willing to go over them in thought, although I do not know why we .eed it. I don't think that there exists a normal man who, instead of saying *'some balls are not red'* would say that *'some non-red objects are not non-ball'*."

"Don't rush to conclusions concerning what is useful and what is not. Just wait until tomorrow and I am sure your opinion will change."

"All right, you can convince me tomorrow, but no lesson should last forever. Some non-logical objects are interesting to me. Some ..."

"Put a stop to that. Some individuals have a glib tongue. See you tomorrow!"

"This means that you will not give me any homework."

"Oh, I nearly have forgotten! No person is infallible. I will give you some homework.

Consider that in everyday language we do not always express categorical propositions the way they appear in the formulae. Your task is to transform some of the sentences which we just now used so that they should correspond to some of the basic forms. In doing so, the truth of the propositions should not, of course, change. Also, write the corresponding basic form beside the sentence."

"Oh, I don't know which sentences you mean and how to do this. Please, help me!"

"Don't you know? Then, let's do it together! First I write down some sentences which we used:

    I. *No lesson should last for ever.*

    II. *Some non-logical objects are interesting to me.*

    III. *Some individuals have a glib tongue.*

    IV. *No person is infallible.*

Now, let's see what kind of things belong to the two groups of objects in the first proposition?"

"We affirm a relation between the *'lessons'* and the *'things which should last for ever'*."

"And what is the relation between them?"

"No lessons are things that should last for ever".

"That's correct! This means that if we symbolize *'lessons'* with letter *A* and the *'things which should last for ever'* with letter *B*, then the form of this proposition is: *'No A are B'*" Now, please, analyze the other propositions (2,3,4) in the same way!"

"In the second proposition a relation is affirmed between *non-logical objects'* and *'things which are interesting to me'*. The logical form of it is this: *'Some non-logical objects are things which are interesting to me'*."

"What is the basic categorical proposition which corresponds to this?"

"It corresponds to the basic form: *'Some A are non-B'*. Where *A* replaces 'things that are interesting to me' and *B* *'logical objects'*."

"That is correct!" What about the third and the fourth propositions?"

"*'Some individuals have a glib tongue'* corresponds to the basic categorical proposition *'Some individuals are individuals with glib tongue'* i. e. *'Some A are B'* where *'A'* means *'individuals'* and *'B'* means *'individuals with glib tongue'*.

'No person is infallible' corresponds to the basic categorica proposition: 'No A are B' where 'A' means 'persons', 'B' means 'persons that are infallible'."

"Your answers were so good that I begin to think that perhaps there are persons who are infallible."

"Oh, thanks! But, please, do not ask me what is the logical form of the proposition 'There are persons who are infallible.'"

Which kitten likes to play with a gorilla?

"Do you know what are the characteristics of a kitten that likes o play with a gorilla?"- I asked Vera.

"No. What strange questions you ask!"

"No? Then I will tell you. From among the following five propositions you will get to know the characteristics of kittens that like to play with gorillas.

1/ *Any kitten that likes fish is not unteachable.*

2/ *All kittens which have short tails do not like to play with gorillas.*

3/ *Every kitten that has whiskers likes fish.*

4/ *No teachable kitten has green eyes.*

5/ *Every kitten without whiskers has a short tail.*

What are the characteristics of a kitten which likes to play with a gorilla?"

Vera took a paper and a pencil. She wrote down the five propositions. She thought for a while, wrote down something, then crossed it out, then wrote again, and at last she stopped.

Kittens that like to play with gorillas do not have short tails. have whiskers, like fish, are teachable and do not have green eyes."

"The solution is good. How did you find out?"

"I have inferred it logically" - she said with a mischievous smile. It seemed she intended it for flattery.

"Tell me your line of reasoning."

"Well, I will tell you. I started out from the second proposition. From this I knew that kittens that like to play with gorillas do not have short tails."

"How did you know this?"

"Well, it is clear, as kittens that have short tails do not like to play with gorillas, the ones which like to play do not have short tails."

"What did you say? Clear? That's not an explanation. Give the reason why it is so, that is, how you know it."

"Look, if kittens that have short tails are not among the ones that like to play with gorillas, there can only be kittens that do not have short tails among the ones that like to play with gorillas. Is it not so?"

"How do you know that?"

"Oh don't bother me! Tell me what you want to me to say."

"I just wanted you to realize that you used the logical law according to which the proposition *'All B are non-A'* is deducible from the form *'No A are B'* because if A things do not belong to B things, (kittens that have short tails are not among the ones that like to play with gorillas) then the B things (kittens that like to play with gorillas) can only belong to *non-A* things (kittens that do not have short tails). This is an inference from one categorical proposition to another categorical proposition. Here you used one of the relationships of which you spoke so disparagingly yesterday. Do you remember?"

"Yes, when we spoke about the categorical propositions that can be deduced from the basic forms."

"Today we are going to speak about inferences in which we infer from two categorical proposition to a third one. You applied such inferences when you stated the other characteristics of kittens that like to play with gorillas and do not have short tails."

"Then please tell me how I have reasoned. I see you know it better than myself do."

"This was precisely my plan for today.
The next thing you got to know was that every kitten that likes to play with a gorilla does not belong among those that have whiskers, wasn't it?"

"Yes, it was."

"You may have reasoned this way:

> *No kittens that likes to play with gorilla has a short tail.*
> *Every kitten without whiskers has a short tail.*

Therefore; *No kitten that likes to play with a gorilla is without whiskers.*

You see, this is such an inference where we infer to the relationship between two classes of things on the basis of the fact that we know their relationship with a third one. To use the former example, we could infer to the relationship between a 'kitten that likes to play with a gorilla' and a 'kitten without whiskers' on the basis of the fact that we know their relation to a 'kitten that has a short tail'. If you replace the 'kittens that like to play with gorillas' with A, the 'kittens with whiskers' with B, and the 'kitten that have short tails' with C, we get the formula of the inference. Which is:

> No A are C
> All non-B are C
> Therefore; No A are non-B

Here we know the relationship of A to C and the relationship non-B to C and from this we infer to the relationship between A and non-B."

"How can you prove this is a correct inference, that is, that this correspondence holds true for any A, non-B, C?"

There are several ways to prove it. I will prove it with the aid of our imaginary chest. For this purpose we have to put more boxes into the chest. I will show you how I have separated C things from non-C things in the chest.

I have put an inner box into each of the former four parts, and I have placed C things there. Thus the non-C things all remain outside of these inner boxes. Now the chest has eight parts:

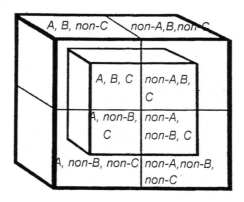

From now on I will represent the chest in a simplified form. Like this:

1.1		3.1
	1.2	3.2
	2.2	4.2
2.1		4.1

It will be somewhat more complicated to denote whether the boxes are empty or not. In order to illustrate the proposition 'All A are B' we have to put 0 into both parts of box 2.

All A are B:

1.1		3.1
	1.2 **O**	3.2
	2.2	4.2
2.1 **O**		4.1

If, however, we wish to illustrate the proposition 'Some A are B', we are not sure whether we should put an asterisk into part 1.1 or 1.2 or perhaps into both. Namely, we do not know whether the things which have both A and B characteristics, have also C characteristics or not. Therefore I will illustrate it like this:

Some A are B:

1.1		3.1
	1.2	3.2
	2.2	4.2
2.1		4.1

Be careful: It does not mean that there is something in both boxes, it only means that there is something in at least one of them.
Show me, please, how you represent the opposition 'No A are C'."

"Here you are:"

No A are C

1.1			3.1
	1.2 O	3.2	
	2.2 O	4.2	
2.1			4.1

"That's right. Now show me how you represent the proposition *'All non-B are C'*."

"It is as follows:"

All non-B are C

1.1			3.1
	1.2	3.2	
	2.2	4.2	
2.1 O		O	4.1

"Now, please combine the two drawings."

"O. K.! It looks like this:"

1.1			3.1
	1.2	3.2	
	2.2 O	O 4.2	
2.1 O		O	4.1

"Can you tell from this diagram what is the relationship between A and *non-B*?"

"Yes, I can. *No A are non-B*, because there is 0 in both 2.1 and 2.2."

"Congratulations! You proved that

> *No A are C*
> *All non-B are non-C*
> *Therefore; No A are non-B*

is a correct inference."

"This is really a chest of wonders! I have proved that *'no kittens that like to play with gorillas are without whiskers'*. This is what we have asserted with the proposition *'no A are non-B'*."

"No, you have not proved exactly that. You have only proved that this proposition follows from the propositions *'No kittens that like to play with gorillas have short tails'* and *'No kittens without whiskers have short tails'*. That is, you have proved that the inference is correct. But the **correctness of the inference** will guarantee the truth of the conclusion only when premises are true. To put it more precisely, you have proved that if the premises we have used in the inference are true, the consequence is also true.

It is the task of logic to verify the correctness of inferences. It is not logic that decides whether the five propositions I have told you at the beginning of our talk are true or not. It is not logic which decides whether there is a kitten with green eyes or not. Logic will only show what we can surely deduce from the propositions, that is, what is true in case the propositions are true."

"But it will also show what we can not deduce from it, that is, what certainly is not true."

„You have gone a bit too far. Logic can verify the incorrectness of some inferences, but at best it can only prove that if the premises are true, some conclusions are not true. But it can not always prove even that. Sometimes it can only prove that a given proposition does not follow from the premises, but apart from this the given proposition may or may not be true."

"Could you tell me examples of both instances?"

"Yes, I can. As regards the first instance, I will tell you a very simple example. We have proved that the proposition *'No A are non-B'* is the consequence of the propositions *'No A are C'* and *'All non-B are C'*. Here we affirm that A is incompatible with *non-B*. If, from the above premises we infer, for example, that *'Some A are non-B'*, that is, that A is compatible with *non-B*, then on the basis of logic we can tell that we did not infer correctly, for we can see that if the premises are true, the proposition *'Some A are non-B'* is not true.

Now let us take an example as regards the second instance, that is, when logic only shows that the given conclusion does not follow from the premises, but may or may not be true.

We have advanced to where you got to know that *'No kittens that like to play with gorillas are without whiskers'*. Let us suppose that you add the following proposition to it: *'All kittens that like fish have whiskers'* and from this you infer that *'All kittens that like to play with gorillas like fish'*. Did you infer correctly in this case?"

"In short, the inference is:

> *No kittens that like to play with gorillas are without whiskers.*
> *All kittens that like fish have whiskers.*
Therefore; all kittens that like to play with gorillas like fish.

The inference seems to be correct, but first I express it by a formula and then I check it. Does it make any difference what I denote with A?"

"Actually it is all the same. But let us agree that A will denote the things of which we state something in the conclusion and that B will denote the things the relationship of which with A we state in the conclusion, and that C will denote the things that occur in both premises, which actually connect A with B."

"Then the formula is as follows:

No A are non-C.
All B are C.
Therefore; All A are B.

I am going to represent the premises in the chest:

No A are non-c

1.1 O			3.1
	1.2	3.2	
	2.2	4.2	
2.1 O			4.1

All B are C

1.1 O			O 3.1
	1.2	3.2	
	2.2	4.2	
2.1			4.1

Now I combine the two drawings!

1.1 O			3.1
	1.2	3.2	
	2.2	4.2	
2.1 O			4.1

"Can you tell from this schedule that 'All A are B'?

"No I cannot, because I have no information whether box 2.2 is empty.
But how on earth is that? I do not remember, but probably I reasoned that way in solving a problem, and you said the solution was good."

"Your solution was really good. But if you reasoned that way, your inference was not correct. I only said that the **solution was good**, that is, had you inferred correctly, the result would have been the same. After all I cannot look into your thoughts. In this case we can say, *'a blind man may hit the mark by chance'*. That is, sometimes you can get correct results through wrong inference, but the trouble is that you can also get a wrong one. That's why it is important to infer correctly. If you inferred like this, I think I know where you made the mistake."

"Where?"

"How did you arrive at; *'All kittens that like fish have whiskers'*?"

"Wait a bit, I will have a look at the paper where I have written down the five premises. I have got it! The third proposition says *'all kittens that like fish are kittens that have whiskers'*."

"Yes, that's right, but you can not find this proposition in the incorrect inference which we have just analyzed, but you can find another one which does not follow from it. The formula which corresponds to the original is *'All C are B'*, but it does not follow from this that *'All B are C'*. Look, I will draw both of them, and you will see the difference between the two propositions.

All C are B

1.1				3.1
	1.2		3.2	
	2.2 O		O 4.2	
2.1				4.1

All B are C

1.1	O			O	3.1
	1.2		3.2		
	2.2		4.2		
2.1					4.1

"This means, that if I inferred like this, not only was my inference incorrect, but even among the premises of the inference was at least one of doubtful truth."

"Sure. You can not infer from the five premises that all kittens that like fish have whiskers. Maybe there is one among them that has no whiskers. All that we know on the basis of the premises about kittens that like fish is that they are teachable and haven't green eyes. We can not infer the other characteristics. I will show its verification at another time.
Now I would like you to draw the conclusion of the following premises by using the chest:

Some problem-solving is entertaining.
All problem-solving needs patience.
Therefore; ?"

"I will try it. I will group the things according to three characteristics. Let:

A = 'problem-solving things'
B = 'entertaining things'
C = 'things the solution of which needs patience'
Then the two propositions are ..."

"Just wait a bit. Order is the essence of things. First let us make clear what you are looking for."

"I am trying to find the conclusion that follows from the premises."

"Try to specify your task more exactly. What do you know? What relationship is not clear from the premises, but can become clear from the conclusion?"

"I know the relationship of *problem-solving things* to the two other groups, but their interrelationship is not mentioned in any of the propositions."

"Right, so you want to state their relationship in the conclusion. Then you'd better call C what you can find in both premises. Mark *problem-solving things'* with C, then *entertaining things'* with A, and the *things the solution of which needs patience'* with B. Now, you can tell the formula!"

"Some C are A.
All C are B.
Now I represent them in the chest.
First, the premise *Some C are A'*:

1.1		3.1
	1.2	3.2	
	2.2*	4.2	
2.1		4.1

I put the asterisk on the line between 1.2 and 2.2 because I did not know in which part I could find the thing that has both A and C characteristic, but it must be at least in one of them.

The second premise is 'All C is B'.
It representation in the chest looks like this:

1.1				3.1
	1.2		3.2	
	2.2 O		O 4.2	
2.1				4.1

Now I combine the two drawings ... It is not so simple, but I have found out what I can infer."

"First finish drawing!"

"Well, but first I have to put the asterisk in another place. That is, both the asterisk and 0 cannot be in box 2.2. The second proposition makes it clear that I have to put the asterisk into box 1.2. We have come to know from the second proposition that box 2.2 is empty. Therefore I combine the two drawings like this:"

1.1				3.1
	1.2 *		3.2	
	2.2 O		O 4.2	
2.1				4.1

"That's correct, and what did you get to know from this regarding the relationship of A to B?"

72

"I got to know that *'Some A are B'* and *'Some B are A'.* In order to know that box 1 is not empty, it is enough to know that either box 1.1 or box 1.2 is not empty."

"Then how does the inference read in the given example?"

"'There are some entertaining things the solution of which needs patience'
and

'There are some things that need patience and they are entertaining.'
This, for example, is fairly entertaining. It is like a puzzle. Please, give me one more example and I will solve it."

"I will tell you a story into which I have hidden an inference. You have to work out how you can formulate the premises and the conclusion exactly. Then you begin to verify it. And I will give you a solution to the problem. Of course, I am not sure that you will choose the same formulation. And I call your attention to the fact that you will find propositions in the example, where we affirm something about a class of things which we have chosen not on the basis of some common characteristics, but about a single specimen. Look at such propositions as *'All A are B'* or *'No A are B'.*

"There is logic in it. When in box 1 I have only one ball and it is red, I can say *'Every ball in box 1 is red'*"

"That is true. If I mark *'the only one ball in box 1'* with *A*, and if i mark *'red thing'* with *B*, the above proposition will correspond - although a little inaccurately - to the formula *'All A are B'.*"

Problem:

<u>The title of the story: the talkative teacher.</u>

The school has received a new teacher. After his first day in class the director asked him what impressions he gained of the students. The teacher thinks that he has won the children's confidence. He resolved to speak with each child in

73

his class. He has spoken only with one of them, who said frankly, that he regularly stole cigarettes from his father.
'Who is this child?' - the director asked.
'I have promised the child that I will keep the content of our talk secret' - said the teacher. 'I think I have not disclosed anything by what I have said.'
The director put up with it and went home. At home he asked his son how he liked the new teacher, his form-master. His son answered:
'He seems to be a nice chap. Just imagine I was the first boy in the class with whom he had a talk.'
The director drew the inference and from this time on he kept careful watch over his cigarettes.

Solutions to the problem:

The only child the teacher talked with regularly stole cigarettes from his father.

My son is the only child the teacher talked with.

Therefore: my son regularly stole cigarettes from his father.

A = my son
B = somebody who regularly stole cigarettes from his father
C = the only child with whom the teacher talked

All C are B
All A are C
Therefore;   *All A are B*

1.1					3.1
	1.2			3.2	
	2.2	O		4.2	
2.1	O				4.1

The inference is correct.

III.

True or Not True?

"Only you could make this big a mess in your room," said John.
"That's not true," said Agatha.
"Why?"
"Why, why? I'll tell you why. If someone states something which doesn't square with reality then his statement isn't true."
"So what you are saying is that I'm a liar."
"That's not what I said. A lie is the deliberate twisting of the truth. A statement which is not true doesn't have to be a lie. Anyway, what you have said doesn't square with reality. I didn't make this mess. So you didn't state the truth: in other words, your statement is false. If you'd like, I'd be happy to quote a few words from Aristotle for you:

'... to say of what is that it is, or of what is not that it is not, is true.'

"Just can't wait to show off that you have studied logic, can you? Seems like anytime I want to talk to you lately, you change the topic to logic. Even you have to admit your room is a pigsty. So what I said wasn't completely wrong. There was some truth in it - one element of it did square with reality."

"You aren't reasoning along the right lines. If you keep on like this you are bound to find some truth in almost any statement. But, quite the contrary! If I were to say that 'the cat in my room is sitting on top of my piano' this statement wouldn't be any truer if I really had a cat and a piano here in my room but the cat were sitting in the armchair. A statement is true only when it is wholly true. Partial truth is still not the truth!"

"And why not! Do you mean to question the philosophical thesis that we can approach absolute truth only through relative truths?"

"You're mixing up two completely different things. Every true statement - no matter whether it's you or me or anyone else who makes it - whether it's about an event connected with everyday life or involves a scientific discovery, is relatively true. That means it's true from a given point of view. But relative truth isn't a mixture of true and false. It contains information which is true when considered alongside given suppositions, and might eventually even be expanded with other information. That's why the postulates of Euclidean geometry, Newtonian physics, etc. are all relatively true. **'True'** and **'false'** - in the sense I mean them - are the possible logical values of a statement. So rest assured that your statement is false. I'm not responsible for this mess. Larry must have struck again, or else there was a stranger in my room."

"One or two of your statements don't square with reality, either. I'm positive Larry didn't strike here. He just called from Eger to say he'd sprained his ankle and he'll have to stay there till next week. He can't even strike out on his own two feet, let alone to have struck around here."

"I hope you're joking."

"Only partly. The verb 'to strike' does have several different meanings. But seriously, the statement *'Larry must have struck here'* is false."

"All right,, I believe you. But that's not what I said. My statement was; *'Larry must have struck again, or else there was a stranger in my room.'* This is a single statement. When someone states something, he presumes it is the truth - or at least he would like others to believe that he considers what he's stating to be true. Considered from the logical point of view every statement, or to use the technical term every proposition, is a thought fixed in a sentence, about which it makes sense to ask whether it's true or not.

Propositions are the logical content in a declarative sentence. The sentence, *'Today is July 18, 1998'* is a declarative sentence, and looked at from the point of view of its logical content, a proposition, since here it makes sense to ask, *'Is it true that today is July 18, 1998?'*. But in the case of imperative sentences like *'Shut the window, please',* it doesn't make sense to ask, *'Is it true that shut the window, please?'* All it makes sense to ask here is whether the given imperative is significant, correct, or meaningful. It wouldn't be significant if there were no windows around, and it wouldn't be meaningful if the only window in the room was closed.

Let's suppose I state the following: *'If today is July, 18, 1980, then it's Friday'.* In linguistics this statement would be known as a declarative sentence, and in logic a proposition. If you took apart this proposition and divided it into its components, you'd find that it contains other propositions. Just what kind of propositions am I talking about? Now here's your chance to give the answer"

"Okay teach! Here are two propositions:

I. *Today is July 18, 1980.*
II. *It's Friday."*

"The statement *'Larry must have struck here, or there was a stranger in my room'* also contains two propositions. It is a compound proposition.
If you like, I can even tell you about all the different kinds of propositions I've studied."

"Am I supposed to be interested in this, or something?"

"Do you like Mastermind?"

"Sure."

"And you like riddles, too, don't you?"

"Sure, I do."

"Would you like to know how your mind must work, to get the right answer?"

"Okay."

"That's why you have to know what the main types of compound propositions are, since a lot of times you use the knowledge of their properties when you make deductions."

"Never get mixed up with a real 'brain'. Alright, I'll listen. But will you play a game of Mastermind with me afterwards?"

"I'll play as much as you want. At least I'll be able to see if you were paying attention to what I said."

"You never change, do you?"

It Is Not True That . . .

"Let's start with negation. Are you ready?"

"Come on, already."

"In a word, then..."

"What's this now? In a word, or in a sentence? You said you were going to state certain things you think are true. But-if I guess right - words in themselves are not statements. You can't ask about plain, individual words whether they are true or not."

"Right you are. But there are cases where 'one word' counts as a statement. Take a language like Hungarian, where one word contains the subject and the predicate rolled into one."

"I knew you must have learned something from hearing your folks speak Hungarian all day. Teach me a little Hungarian!"

"Well, for example, there's 'I love you' - 'Szeretlek'. That's one word in Hungarian, but it contains the subject and the predicate, so it counts as a sentence."

"Do you really mean it? You love me?"

"That's not what I said. That was just an example of a proposition - of a grammatical structure. You were farthest from my mind. But I guess you're not worth talking to."

"What d'ya mean, not worth talking to? I just learned how to tell the difference between the logical content of words and sentences. Words by themselves are not sufficient to be either true or false. **'True'** or **'false'** is the possible logical truth value of a proposition. A proposition is the logical content of a declarative sentence. Am I pretty much on the right track?"

"Uh-huh, but you also have to know that propositions can be divided into two main groups - simple and compound. When we break down the compound proposition, it contains one or more component propositions. But be careful, since not all propositions we call compound have propositions as their components. The only time a proposition is called **compound** is when you can decide its truth value entirely on the basis of the truth or falsity of its constituent propositions."

"That sound complicated. Give me an example or two."

"All right - *'Tom got a cold from sleeping without mittens'*. Break down the proposition, and you'll get two propositions:

    I. *Tom got a cold.*

    II. *Tom slept without mittens."*

"But it doesn't actually matter whether you know that the first and second propositions are true - you still don't know whether the cause and effect relationship the propositions puts forward is true.

Or take another example - *'Peter thinks John loves Mary.'* If you split up this proposition, you'll find that you can ask whether a part of it is true. That is, you'll see it contains the proposition, *'John loves Mary'*. But the truth or falsity of this proposition has no impact on the truth value of the overall proposition."

"Sure. If John loves Mary that doesn't tell me whether Peter really believes the situation is true. And if it's not true that John loves Mary, Peter might still think that John does love Mary. But maybe the problem here is that if I break down the propositions, *'Peter thinks that John loves Mary'*, only one of the sections is a proposition, while the other, *'Peter thinks that'*, isn't."

"Not exactly. In some compound propositions, there is only one component proposition. You just used a little while ago - *'It's not true that John loves Mary.'* This is the negation of the proposition, *'John loves Mary'*. If you know the truth value of the component proposition, then you can come up with the truth value of the negation, too. *'It's not true that John loves Mary'* is false if *'John loves Mary'* is true. But if *'John loves Mary'* is false, the negation is true.

Along with the expression, *'it's not true that'* there are other phrases you can use. For example, *'John doesn't love Mary'* is also the negation of the proposition, *'John loves Mary'*. The negation of the proposition, *'I don't have a piano in my room'* is the phrase, *'I have a piano in my room.'* Now tell me when the proposition, *'It's not true that John doesn't love Mary'* would be true."

"It would be true if John loved Mary."

"Right. Any proposition can be negated as much as you like. The rule in logic says that any odd-numbered negation changes the value of the original proposition to the opposite value (if you like, it changes true to false and false to true), and the truth value of any even-numbered negation corresponds to the truth value of the original proposition."

"So if I say, *'It's not true that it's not true that it's not true that you aren't beautiful';* that's a quadruple negation, and it would mean that you're beautiful."

"Take my advice and don't monkey around with such complicated propositions. If you use those in everyday speech people will think there's something wrong with you. If they weren't aware you were doing logic, they might even call an ambulance. There's no need to express something in so complicated a way when you can just say it plainly."

"Then why have rules like this in logic at all? Is that very logical?"

"Sure it is. Logic includes more than just the forms of thought people usually use when they reason. It attempts to set up possible forms of thought. It tries to account for all the possibilities. On top of it, we have no way of knowing what the maximum number of negations would be that, say, the everyday person uses, and what is the number that has practically never been used. Logic isn't really concerned with the problem anyway.

Hey, know what? Let's get out Mastermind! Let's play a round right now! I just realized that we'll make a lot more use of negative propositions in the game. I'm curious to know if you too will be able to notice them."

"Now that's a neat idea! All right, let's play. I'll be the code-maker," - volunteered John. "The only problem is that we don't have a Mastermind board."

"Oh this is no problem. I will give you instructions, how to play it without a board. You don't need anything more than a sheet of paper and a pencil."

Here are the instruction:

Instruction to the Mastermind game

Mastermind usually is played on a game-board like the one you see here:

				O	O	O	O
V	O O	O O		O	O	O	O
IV	O O	O O		O	O	O	O
III	O O	O O		O	O	O	O
II	O O	O O		O	O	O	O
I	O O	O O		O	O	O	O
				1	2	3	4

The basic object of the Mastermind game is to guess a secret code consisting of colored pegs. The game has different versions. One is as follows:

One player, known as the Code-maker, secretly puts 4 colored pegs, i.e. code-pegs, in a certain order behind the holes shielded from the other player's view. Use any combination of the 6 colors. Use 2 or more code pegs of the same color if you wish. The other player, known as the Code-breaker, tries to duplicate the exact colors and positions of the secret code. Each time the Code-breaker places a row of code pegs (they are then left in position throughout the game), the Code-maker must give information by placing the black and white key pegs in the key peg holes alongside the code pegs, or by leaving holes vacant.

A black key peg is placed in any of the 4 key peg holes for every code peg which is the same color and in exactly the same position as one of the code pegs in the shielded holes.

A white key peg is placed in any of the 4 key peg holes which is matched in color but not in position.

When the Code-breaker duplicates the secret code, the Code-maker places 4 black key pegs and reveals the hidden code.

We can use diagrams, with the following abbreviations, instead of a game-board:

CODE PEGS:
Red	= R
Green	= G
Violet	= V
Purple	= P
Blue	= B
Yellow	= Y

KEY PEGS:
| White | = O |
| Black | = X |

I, II, III, IV, V; are rows of subsequent hypotheses as well as feedback from the Code-maker.

1, 2, 3, 4; designate the order of the code pegs.

"OK!", - said Agatha "let's play this version of Mastermind."

This was the game John and Agatha played:

			1	2	3	4
			R	B	G	G
V	X X X X		R	B	G	G
IV	X X		R	B	P	P
III	X		R	V	R	V
II	O O		V	Y	B	R
I	O X		P	V	G	R

As they were playing, Agatha thought out her moves. After playing the second row she said:

"Red isn't in the fourth place"

After the third row she said:

"*It's not true that both red and violet are in the code.*"

After playing the fourth row she said:

"*Purple isn't in the code either.*"

And then added:

"*The hidden code is none other than red, blue, green, green.*"

"Okay," said John. "You hit the code."

"I hope you see how negative propositions helped me in guessing the right answer."

"Sure I do. But how'd you get the solution?"

"After the first row I assumed that the proposition, *'Red is in the fourth place'* was true. After the second row I realized that this assumption was false. So I was sure that red wasn't in the fourth place. You see, this proposition was the negation of the previous one, and the fact that the previous one had been false made this one true. Then I assumed that there were two violets or reds in the code."

"Why did you assume that?"

"I assumed that I had gotten the feedback for red and violet in the first and second rows. If red and violet were in, then purple, yellow, green and blue had to be out."

"So what did you know from the third row?"

"I decided that it's not true that *'There are two violets or two reds in the code.'* "

"You mean you assumed that there weren't two violets and there weren't two reds?"

"That's right. That's the same as what I just said."

"Later I'd like to ask you a little more about that. But for now, tell me what you found out after the fourth row."

"After the fourth row I was positive that purple couldn't be in the code either."

"But that isn't a true statement!"

"What makes it not true?"

"The simple reason is that the statement, *'It's not true that purple couldn't be in the code'* is true. You taught me that I could cancel the double negation, and probably simplify facts a little by saying, *'purple can be in the code.'* So the code could just as well have been yellow, violet, purple, purple."

"Hey, you're right! In this case purple and violet were hits as far as color in the first row, and violet was in the right place. In the second row, yellow and violet were hits as far as color, and in the third row, one of the violets was in the right place. In the fourth row, the two purples were in the right position.
The moral of the story is that you can make discoveries using false propositions - with a little bit of luck."

"I agree. Anyway, you were also wrong in saying that if purple weren't in the code, then the hidden code would be none other than red, blue, green, and green. It might just as well have been red, blue, green, and blue. Now what sort of lessons in logic do you want to draw from this?"

"Well, let's start off by discussing the fact that you're making fun of me - though that's not a lesson in logic."

"What hurt your feelings this time?"

"My feelings aren't hurt. But I'm not going to teach you anymore. It'd be just like pulling the rug from under my own two feet."

Don't Contradict Yourself!

John said good- bye. Just as he was leaving, Agatha called after him.

"Come by tomorrow, too! We can play another game ot Mastermind so we can analyze it logically."

"Don't you see what you're saying is self-contradictory?" asked John.

"Why's that?"

"You already said you wouldn't teach me anymore and now you're saying tomorrow you want to analyze a game of Mastermind with me. Do you call that not teaching me, or what?"

"That's teaching, all right. But I didn't get involved up in a contradiction. When I said I wouldn't teach you anymore, I meant that the teaching was over for today. *Today, the 11th of September, I won't be teaching you anymore'* and *'Tomorrow, the 12th of September, I'll teach you'* aren't incompatible propositions."

"Then next time put it a little more precisely."

"You're the one to talk. You, who, I just bet, hasn't heard of the principle of contradiction. Or maybe you do know it?"

"I can't say I do. Go on and tell me, so we can make up."

"I won't make up with you, but I'll tell you anyway. The principle of contradiction says that, in sound reasoning, we shouldn't state propositions that are incompatible with one another."

"But which propositions are considered **incompatible?**"

"Two propositions are incompatible when one can't be true if the other is, and the other way round."

"So they contradict each other."

"Be careful! Logic makes a distinction between **contradictory** and **contrary** propositions. Both contradictory and contrary propositions belong to the category of **incompatible propositions**. Contradictory propositions are distinguished by the fact that, although they can't be true together, one of them must be true. Take these pairs of contradictory propositions, for instance: *'Today is Wednesday'* and *'Today is not Wednesday'.* Or *'Every book is entertaining'* and *'Some books are not entertaining'.*

Contrary propositions can't be true together, but both of them can be false. Take the pair, *'I understand everything that the teacher is explaining'* and *'I don't understand a thing that the teacher is explaining'* Both may be false if the truth is, say, there are things in the teacher's explanation that I do understand and there are some other things which I don't understand.

But whether you're talking about contradictory or contrary propositions, after stating one of a pair of such propositions it would be a mistake in logic to state the other, since they can't be true together.

The principle of contradiction can also be violated when someone makes a statement, and then later on says something which doesn't agree with the consequences of the first statement."

"Run that by me again. This is one case where *'My teacher explained something I don't understand'* would be true."

"Don't get impatient. Here's an example which will help make everything clear.

> *Mr. Fibber's secretary is calling one of his clients to make excuses for her boss:*
> *'Hello, this is Mr.Fibber's secretary,' she says.*
> *'Mr.Fibber, unfortunately, can't attend the meeting you called, since he's been called away on urgent business. He is out of town and we don't expect him back until tomorrow. He thanks you for your kind understanding, and wants to know whether it's okay if we deliver the commission next week instead.'*
> *'Did Mr. Fibber receive our letter?'*
> *'That I can't tell you. But I'll ask him now -he's right here beside me.'*
> *'And tell me, where are you calling from?'*
> *'Me? From downtown. Why do you ask?'* "

"No need to explain the example. Now I see what you mean Thanks for teaching me, Agatha."

"You're welcome."

"So you admit you were teaching me?"

"Yes, I do."

"Now I've got you! I can really show you've contradicted yourself. You said that you were through teaching me for today, and you went right on teaching."

"Whoa, pal - that's not a logical contradiction. Here we aren't talking about the opposition of two incompatible propositions; this is a contradiction between words and facts."

"You're always finding some way to extricate yourself. Are you trying to tell me that it's okay for a contradiction to exist between words and deeds?"

"No, that would be going too far. All I wanted to say is that not all contradictions are logical. There are other kinds, too - like dialectical contradictions, which are intrinsic features of development rather than mistakes or inconsistencies."

"Now don't tell me that your contradiction was one of those" interrupted John. "I wouldn't go so far as to say that. I admit that contradiction between words and deeds is as much of an inconsistency as logical contradiction is. But my mistake didn't violate the logical principle of contradiction, since this stipulation only applies to statements. That's all I wanted to say and I'm finished for today."

It's a good thing this talk went on so late at night, since Agatha was able to keep her word, even under the greatest duress. She managed to steer clear of any contradiction for the rest of the entire day.

So What?

"I'm not angry with you anymore" said Agatha, next time she saw John.

"Why were you angry in the first place?" he asked.

"'Cause you were trying to prove that I don't think logically all the time even though I study logic."

"Why? Isn't that the truth?"

"Sure it is. I realized it is quite natural though. Even someone who knows English grammar can still make grammatical mistakes. Mathematicians know lots of things and they still make wrong calculations. I've only been studying logic for a very short time, so why should my thinking be perfect? And who knows - even you, who've just begun to study logic, could be thinking more logically than I am sometimes. Why should it matter if a student gets better than his teacher, anyway?"

"Do all these flattering remarks mean you want to go on teaching me?"

"You guessed it - my word had a double purpose" said Agatha, smiling.

"Okay, then I don't mind" - said John, resigning himself to being a student.

"Last time, we were talking about negation. You already learned that by negating a simple proposition you get a compound proposition - a **negation**. But along with negating simple propositions, you can also negate some propositions which are already compound. Negating a compound proposition, then, is also an instance of double negation. For instance, the negation of the negative proposition, *'John isn't a very nice guy'* is the proposition, *'It's not true that John isn't a very nice guy'*."

"You're trying to butter me up, to get me pay better attention to you - said John

Agatha went on:

"You can also negate a proposition which is a compound made up of several propositions. Examples of this type of negative proposition would include the following;

'It's not true that there are two violets and reds in the code'."

"It's a good thing you brought up that proposition. I wanted to ask you something about it. Do you remember when you said that

'It's not true that there are two violets or two reds in the code'
was the same thing as saying that

'there aren't two violets in the code, and there aren't two reds in the code'.
Why do you think that both say the same thing? After all, they're two different sentences."

"Actually, they're only identical from a certain point of view - one of them can be true at the same time the other is, and if one of them is false, then so is the other. That is, they aren't identical because the first is the negation of a compound proposition, and the second is a compound proposition made up of the negation of two simple propositions."

"Run that by me again. I don't see what you are saying."

"In the first instance I'm negating a compound proposition, and so that makes it a negation. In the second instance we're dealing with a compound proposition where the components are negative propositions. It would help you to understand better if you let me tell you about the different kinds of compound propositions which are made up of two or more propositions."

"Alright. You won't hear a peep out of me."

"I'd rather hear you make a peep - then at least I'd know what I have to explain better. But don't expect to understand everything in the first minute! Wait a little bit.
As we already said, each proposition conveys just a small amount of information - just like a raindrop. By itself one drop of rain doesn't make a storm, but if we have a whole cloudburst of raindrops - there you go!"

"Oh, oh - get ready for the storm! The storm of words."

"First let's talk about **conjunctions**. Do you remember that detective story we were watching on TV? - you know, the part where the detective realizes that the murderer broke the dead captain's wristwatch. The detective goes around to all the suspects, holds up a running watch to their ears, and says *'This watch belonged to the* captain.' Most of the people there responded by saying 'so what?' But one of them said, 'The watch is running'."

"Now it's my turn to ask the same thing - so what?"

"The same day I'd been watching that detective story I was studying about conjunctions - propositions which express the simultaneous existence of two or more facts. We generally ask the question, 'so what?', when we've been told about a fact and are waiting to get the rest of the facts which exist side by side with the first. Those who answered the detective by saying 'so what?', didn't feel that the statement, 'This watch belonged to the captain' expressed anything important - anything essential. They were expecting the detective to join this with another proposition, tack on the conjunction 'and' and add it to another proposition."

"I suppose you mean that the proposition
'This watch belongs to the captain and this watch is running'
is a compound proposition. "

"That's right. Here is another example of a conjunction:
'Steve was watching TV and all of a sudden it went dead.'
This is made up of the conjunction of the propositions:
1. 'Steve was watching TV.'
and
2. 'All of a sudden the TV went dead.'
It expresses that the two situations existed at the same time. **A conjunctive proposition, or more simply a conjunction is true if and only if all its component propositions are true.**"

"Now I see what you mean.
'Steve was watching TV and all of a sudden the TV went dead'
isn't true if one of the situations didn't actually happen. It's only true when both the situations
'Steve is watching TV'
and
'all of a sudden it went dead'
hold true at the same time."

"Yes, and conjunctions are frequently expressed with the word 'and'."

"Are there other ways to express them?"

"Uh-huh. The words *'but'*, *'though'* and *'yet'* are also used for expressing conjunctions. For example, the propositions,

'Peter is a hard worker, but Eve is more hard-working than he is',

as well as,

'Liz always does well on her exams, though she doesn't study very much'

are true when both their component propositions are true. And do you know what propositions are contained in the conjunction, 'Liz always does well on her exams, though she doesn't study very much'?"

"'Liz always does well on her exams',

and

'Though she doesn't study very much.'"

"Wrong. *'Though she doesn't study very much'* isn't a proposition. First of all, we've already said that the word 'though' connects propositions - so it doesn't go with either of the component propositions. Second of all, even if you had answered, *'She doesn't study very much'*, that wouldn't have been right either. You can't ask whether this proposition is true in and of itself, since it's truth depends on whom you're talking about. The second proposition is actually, *'Liz doesn't study a lot'*. The word, *'Liz'*, was only left out the first time for the sake of linguistic economy - since there would be no confusion over whom the statement was referring to. But if you want to analyze the component propositions of a conjunction logically, you have to replace what's been left out of the grammatical structure, but would otherwise be there logically. I know this seems like a minor point - but unless someone calls it to our attention, we're bound to make mistakes.

Now here's another example:

'My sister wants a black and white cat'.

Try to figure out how many components this proposition has."

"The first :

'My sister wants a black cat'.

The second:

'My sister wants a white cat'.

Wait a minute! Something's not right here. She doesn't want a black cat and she doesn't want a white cat. She doesn't want two cats. What does she want? She wants one 'black and white cat!'"

"Of course, that is what she wants. The *'and'* here is not used for a conjunction of two propositions. *'And'* is used for more than just conjunctions. Just one more example. In the proposition

'Peter and Paul are neighbors',

'and' expresses the relation between two people; Peter and Paul, rather than between two situations

Why don't we get out Mastermind now? I'd like to use it to explain something to you."

"Let's get at it! I'm always ready to play a game of Mastermind." Agatha put the following graph on the board:

III.	X	R	V	Y	G
II.	-	B	P	B	P
I.	X	G	P	B	P

"Now tell me what you know from the second row," - she asked John.

"Blue and purple aren't in the code," he said.

"Now tell me what you know after playing the third row."

"*'Red, violet, and yellow aren't in the code.'* I know this from having only gotten the feedback for green (after playing the second row) in the first row. This made it quite clear that there are four greens in the hidden code."

"*'There is no blue and no purple in the code',*
is a conjunction joining two negative propositions.

'There's no red, no yellow, and no violet in the code',
is the conjunction of three negations."

"I see. *'Blue isn't in the code'* is the negation of the proposition, *'Blue's in the code.'* Or *'Purple's not in the code'* is the negation of the proposition, *'Purple's in the code'.* But what's so fantastic about that? It's so obvious."

"Do you remember when I said that you have to distinguish the negation of a compound proposition from the negation of the propositions it contains?
Now tell me what the difference is between the following propositions:

1. *It's not true that blue's in the code, and it's not true that purple's in the code.*
2. *It's not true that blue's in the code, but purple's in the code*
3. *It's not true that blue and purple are in the code.*

Now I'm going to show you the difference on the Mastermind board:

1.

-		B	P	B	P

2.

-		B	G	B	G
X		B	P	B	P

3.

O		B	P	B	G

Number one is an example of the conjunction of two negative propositions. To put it another way you could say 'Neither blue nor purple is in the code'.

In number two the negation only concerns the first part of the conjunction. This is a conjunction where one of the component propositions is a negative proposition, while the other isn't a compound proposition.

In number three you have negated the conjunction. You denied that blue and purple are in the code together. One of them might be in the

code, but it's just as possible that neither of them is. The only thing that can't happen is that both would be true.
Now are you convinced that to negate a compound proposition is not the same as negating its components separately?"

"Just a minute, I don't see it yet. Let's get out the Mastermind board again.

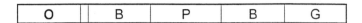

| O | B | P | B | G |

This was the situation that corresponded to the third proposition. In this case, I'm not sure that the second proposition is true, and I'm not sure about the first proposition, either. Alright. That's all I need to go on. Now I see that they are not true in the same situations, since the truth of the second and the first doesn't necessarily follow from the truth of the third."

"In logic when discussing compound propositions we replace the simple propositions or those whose compounds we aren't examining in the given analysis with symbols. The letters $p, q, r...$ etc., are usually used for this purpose.
In addition to being a kind of shorthand, these symbols are also useful because they make what we want to say much more obvious. This is just like when little kids learn to count. At first it helps them a lot when their teacher says, *'In one hand I have an apple and in the other I have two. Now tell me how many apples one apple and two apples make?'*
But by the time they get to first grade in grammar school children have to start getting used to the fact that quantitative relations are separated from what they actually resemble in reality. That's when they start to hear the question. *'How much are one and two?'* Then they begin to learn the special mathematical symbols for quantity, as well as for the operations performed with these quantities, such as addition, subtraction, multiplication, equivalence, etc.
Well then, logic also follows similar procedures. A conjunction made up of two propositions is written like this:

$$p \wedge q$$

Just as the cross is the mathematics sign for addition, the little upside down letter 'v' symbolizes that the conjunction is made up of the propositions *p* and *q*.

When we want to negate a proposition, we put a line over the proposition we want to negate. The negation of proposition *p* is written $\bar{p}$. The negation of the whole conjunction $p \wedge q$ is written

$$\overline{p \wedge q}$$

Now let's use the language of logic to describe the three compound propositions we were discussing above. These included two simple propositions:

If p will stand for *'Blue's in the code.'*

   q will stand for *'Purple's in the code.'*

Then the first proposition (*'It's not true that blue's in the code, and it's not true that purple's in the code'*) would look like this:

$$\bar{p} \wedge \bar{q}$$

The second proposition (*'It's not true that blue's in the code, while purple's in the code'*) would read:

$$\bar{p} \wedge q$$

And the third proposition (*'It's not true that blue and purple are in the code'*) would read:

$$\overline{p \wedge q}$$

How much clearer the difference between the three becomes when we use the language of logic to express them!"

"Oh, oh! I've just remembered I haven't done a bit of homework for tomorrow!"

"Then let's stop till next time. I'll come over to your house at 5 o'clock tomorrow or the day after."

Either/or

"Hi, John - I've been expecting you. I've already got the Mastermind board all set up!"

"How did you know I was coming?"

"Don't you remember? The day before yesterday you told me that you would come *'tomorrow or the day after at five o'clock'*. Since you didn't come yesterday, I was positive you were coming today. You're a man of your word."

"Oh, yeah - I forgot I promised. Now let's have a look at your Mastermind board."

"I've already got something on the board:

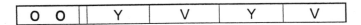

Now tell me - would a player be thinking along the right lines if, after getting this information, he were to state 'yellow or violet is in the code'?"

"But they aren't mutually exclusive! Both can be in the code at the same time."

"That's right, both yellow and violet can be in the code. By the way, why couldn't you have been coming both yesterday and today?"

"Why couldn't I have been? What are you getting at?"

"You're using the word 'or' in the same way as my imaginary player is. In logic this type of proposition is known as a **disjunction**. The disjunction of two propositions is written with a small letter '∨' between them. For example, the disjunction of the proposition p and q would read:

$$p \vee q$$

A disjunction is true when at least one of its component propositions i.e. one of its disjuncts is true. But it's also true when more than one of it's component propositions are true. Going back to the previous example, the proposition *'Yellow or violet is in the code'* is true in the following cases:

1. *Yellow is in the code and violet isn't.*
2. *Yellow isn't in the code and violet is.*
3. *Yellow is in the code and violet is in the code.*

It is false only in this case:

4. *Yellow isn't in the code, and violet isn't in the code."*

"You can also negate a disjunctive proposition.

'It's not true that p or q' = $\overline{(p \vee q)}$,

is true in the situation where neither *p* nor *q* is true. So the negation of the proposition,

'Yellow or violet is in the code'

is the same as the proposition

'It's not true that yellow or violet are in the code.'

Another way of putting this might be

'Neither yellow nor violet is in the code'.

Do you see an interesting connection here?"

"Why? What were you thinking?"

"That the proposition,

'Neither yellow nor violet is in the code'

is the same as the conjunction,

'Yellow isn't in the code and violet isn't in the code', $= \overline{p} \wedge \overline{q}$,

and its truth corresponds to the truth value of the proposition: $\overline{p \vee q}$."

"Ahah! The truth value of the negation of the disjunction is the same as the truth value of the conjunction of the negation of its components:"

$$\overline{p \vee q} = \overline{p} \wedge \overline{q}$$

"You put that very professionally. Now let's put one more row on the board.

II.

-		P	Y	P	Y
O O		Y	V	Y	V

I.

The codemaker didn't give any feedback for the second row, so there was no hit in color. What does this leave you to think?"

"That violet is in the code."

"Your argument was similar to the one I made when I decided you were coming today. So if I know that one of two situations has to hold and I also know that one of them doesn't hold then it has to be true that the other holds.

Or using the language of logic, q follows from the two propositions $p \vee q$ and $\bar{p}$. Expressed as a schema it would look like this:

$$\frac{p \vee q}{\bar{p}}$$

Therefore; q

This is a correct argument schema made on the basis of disjunction."

"So if I inferred p from the propositions $p \vee q$ and $\bar{q}$, that would be just as correct, wouldn't it?"

"Right. But to infer $\bar{q}$ from $p \vee q$ and p wouldn't be correct and to infer $\bar{p}$ from $p \vee q$ and q also wouldn't be correct."

"So if I had come yesterday, it wouldn't have followed that I was not coming today, because I could have come both days. If you said

'Today or tomorrow I would like to teach you logic'

and you taught me today, then it doesn't follow from this that tomorrow you don't want to teach me anymore."

"You're thinking so logically! This must be the influence of my teaching or you bumped your head at birth."

"The two don't have to be mutually exclusive. But look, either you're going to pick on me or you're going to teach me something."

"There you go again - if I'm right, you just used the word 'or' in another sense. What you wanted to state, I guess, is that the two are mutually exclusive. In that case your statement would be false if both existed at the same time. Your statement is a proposition expressing incongruity, or to put it another way - it's an **exclusion**. Here are some other examples of this type of proposition.

'Someone may be a designated driver or he may drink at the party'.

If the Ponsonby Rugby Club is playing Marist Rugby Club then the following exclusion would be true:

'Either the Ponsonby Rugby Club is going to win or Marist Rugby Club is going to win'."

"That's not true. The game could win up a tie."

"Sure, it could be a tie. But all I wanted to say is that the situations are mutually exclusive - they can't both be true at the same time. It wasn't the point to list possibilities where one has to hold, while at the same time only one could hold. If the game wound up a tie (if neither of the two situations actually hold) the statement of their exclusivenes would still be true. The party is a good example of this. If someone doesn't drink at the party and doesn't drive after the party, the fact that drinking and driving are incompatible is still true. Your objection would be justified if I had used the word *'or'* in the above example as an **exclusive disjunction**. So there is a third meaning of the word *'or'*. In the case of exclusive disjunction, the proposition is true only when one and only one of it's component propositions is true."

"Can you give me an example?"

"O. K...

'The triangle in question is either right, acute or obtuse'.
This is made up of three propositions:

1. The triangle in question is right.

2. The triangle in question is obtuse,

3. The triangle in question is acute.

If you like, I can show you the difference between 'exclusion' and 'exclusive disjunction' on the Mastermind set.

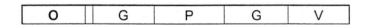

O		G	P	G	V

In this example, the exclusion *'Either green or purple is in the code'* is true. You can see the green and purple can't be there together. But it might also be the case that neither of them is there. If you find out somehow that green is in the code, then you can correctly conclude that purple isn't.

In this case you infer on the basis of the following principle: when you already know that one of them does hold, then you can conclude that the other one (or the rest) does not hold.

The logical symbol for exclusion is a perpendicular line drawn between the mutually exclusive propositions. For example ·

$$p \mathbin{/} q$$

means that p excludes q.

So if I know that p / q, and I also know that p holds, then it follows from this that q. Written in schema:

$$p / q$$
$$p$$

Therefore; $\overline{q}$

This would also go for the situation where p / q and q holds The correct conclusion is $\overline{p}$."

"But your inference would be incorrect if you inferred from p / q and from $\overline{p}$, that q holds or else that p follows from the premises p / q and $\overline{q}$."

"Let's see what that looks like on the Mastermind board.

II.	-	B	Y	R	G
I.	O	G	P	G	V

When I didn't get any feedback for the second row, I knew that green wasn't in the code, but from this and the first row, it didn't follow that purple was in the code. Purple might not be in the code either. But it's now more plausible that purple is in the code."

"You're right. But in all the inferences I've studied about, whenever the premises were true, then the conclusions derived from them were also necessarily true. I've also heard about probability logic but I haven't studied about it yet.

Now I'll put an example on the game board of when an exclusive disjunction with two components would be true."

I.	O	B	G	B	G

"I see. This is when the statement,

'Either blue or green is in the code'

would be true.

This means that one and only one of them is in the code. And how is exclusive disjunction written in logic?"

"You put an upside down triangle between the component propositions, like this:

$$p \triangledown q$$

If you know that there are two situations which are in an exclusive disjunction relationship and you know that one of these situations holds, then you can infer that the other doesn't hold. The schema of the arguments based on exclusive disjunction relationship look like this:

$p \triangledown q$	$p \triangledown q$
p	$\bar{p}$
Therefore; $\bar{q}$	Therefore; q

$p \triangledown q$	$p \triangledown q$
q	$\bar{q}$
Therefore; $\bar{p}$	Therefore; p

"So, by using the above example, if I know from the second row that blue is in the code, then I can infer that green isn't. And if I know that blue isn't in the code, then I can infer that green is, etc."

"What do you mean by 'etc.'?"

"The 'etc.' first of all means that if I know that green is in the code, then I know that blue isn't: If I know that green isn't in the code, then I know that blue is. Second of all, the 'etc.' means 'more to come', but more later on, 'cause I've got to run. Either I leave now, or I don't get to my elective course on time, That was an exclusive disjunction."

"No, it wasn't. It was an exclusion. One thing's sure. If you don't leave now you won't get there, and the only way you can get there is by leaving. But you could leave and still not get there on time. The bus might not come, for example. But now you really do have to hurry!

Take these problems with you. I'll give you a crib sheet with the answers so you can check and see whether you answered everything correctly."

COMPOUND PROPOSITION	TRUE	FALSE
Negation symbol: - /written above the component proposition/	If the component proposition is false	If the component proposition is true
Conjunction /unifying proposition/ symbol: ∧ /written between the component propositions/	If all the component propositions are true	If one or more of the component propositions are true
Disjunction /permissibly alternative proposition/ symbol: ∨ /written between the component propositions/	If at least one of the component propositions is true	If all the component propositions are false
Exclusion /incongruity/ symbol: / /written between the component propositions/	If at least one of the component propositions is false /or the entire proposition is false/	If all the propositions are true
Exclusive Disjunction /exclusively alternative proposition/ symbol: ∇ /written between the component propositions/	If one of the component propositions is true and the other false	If both of the propositions are true or false

Problems

1. Which of the following sentences express a compound proposition:

(a) *Let them eat cakes!*

(b) *The door is closed but the window is opened.*

(c) *Roger told me that one red peg is in the code.*

(d) *Peter Piper picked a peck of pickled peppers.*

2. What is the meaning of *'or'* in the following compound proposition?

"Either the well was very deep, or she fell very slowly, for she had plenty of time as she went down to look about her, and to wonder what was going to happen." (Lewis Carroll: Alice in Wonderland)

3. How many components can you find in the following compound propositions? Symbolize them, using capital letters to abbreviate the simple propositions involved:

(a) *"Alice had not the slightest idea what Latitude was, or Longitude either, but she thought they were nice grand words to say."* (Lewis Carroll: Alice in Wonderland)

(b) *I walked home*
in the velvet of the night's vibration,
jasmines
applauding in a warm soft wind,
my soul a dreaming jungle,
and men slept in the streets. (From the poem 'Ode' by A. József)

Problems solution

1. Compound proposition: (b)
2. (a) disjunction
3. (a)

Alice had not the slightest idea what Latitude was = p
Alice had not the slightest idea what Longitude was = q
She thought they were nice grand words to say = r

$$\overline{(p \lor q)} \land r$$

(b)

I walked home in the velvet of the night's vibration = p
Jasmines applauding in a warm soft wind = q
My soul a dreaming jungle = r
Men slept in the streets = z

$$p \land q \land r \land z$$

Curiosity killed the cat

"The world is full of coincidences!" - said John a few days later, when he went over to Agatha's after school.

"Why? What happened?"

"Would you believe? We were talking about the same things in my elective class at school as you and I were the day before."

"You mean, about the different types of compound propositions? In your computer elective course?"

"Uh-huh, but we were talking about a different aspect than the one you studied. We were discussing the history of the development of computers. Have you ever heard of the 'logic of electric circuits'?"

"No, I have no idea what that is."

"The **logic of electric circuits** is the underlying theory behind computers. It developed at the beginning of the century, when the similarities were discovered between electric circuits and certain laws of logic."

"Which laws of logic are you talking about? I'm really curious about it."

"Curiosity killed the cat. If you're curious, then you'll wind up just like the cat."

"Then I'll quit being curious. And keep your information to yourself."

"There you go again with your whining. Whining also kills cats."

"I've got nothing common with cats. Anyway, at least I can appreciate the meaning of the compound proposition:

'If you're curious, you'll wind up just like the cat.'

The consequent can still be true, even when the antecedent doesn't hold."

"Slow down there! I don't get a word of what you said. Would you explain that, please?"

"Are you curious?"

"Yes."

"Then you'll wind up like the cat."

"Stop monkeying around, will you? Get to the point."

"Your statement,

'If you're curious you'll wind up just like the cat'
is what is known as a **conditional proposition**, or **implication**. This format proposition is almost always expressed with the words: *if ... then*. But the *'then'* is sometimes left out of expressions in daily language, leaving the antecedent to be separated from the consequent only by a comma. So the expression which comes immediately after the *'if'* is called the **antecedent**, while the one after the *'then'* is known as the **consequent**. An implication is written like this:

$$p \rightarrow q$$

p stands for the antecedent, the arrow for the implicative relationship, and q for the consequent. **An implication is false when the antecedent holds (that is when p is true) and the consequent (that is, *q*) is false.** So your statement would be false if I were curious but didn't wind up just like the cat.
Or to give you another example, the proposition,

'If the weather is nice tomorrow, then Mary is going on a trip'
would be false if the weather were nice tomorrow and Mary didn't go on a trip."

"But say tomorrow the weather wasn't nice and Mary still went on a trip (in other words, the antecedent didn't hold but the consequent did), then your proposition would be false."

"No it wouldn't. All I said was that it's not true that the antecedent holds and the consequent doesn't hold. The truth value of the proposition $p \rightarrow q$ is the same as the truth value of the

proposition $\overline{p \land \bar{q}}$. So you see now, that's the same thing as saying: *'it's not true that p and $\bar{q}$ hold together'*.
Here's another example;

'If it rains, the sidewalk will get wet.'
What am I stating here?"

"*'It's not true that it will rain and the sidewalk won't get wet'.*"

"But this statement doesn't imply that if the sidewalk gets wet then it's raining. Notice that, before, I didn't affirm that

> *'If the weather is nice tomorrow, then and only then, is Mary going on a trip.'*

This would be another type of compound proposition. It would be an **equivalence**. You can split an equivalence into two implications, like this:

> *'If the weather is nice tomorrow, then Mary is going on a trip',*

and

> *'If Mary goes on a trip tomorrow, then the weather will be nice'.*

When I state an implication I'm asserting that the consequent will hold when the antecedent does. In other words, that if the antecedent is true, you can conclude the truth of the consequent.

You probably didn't mean to say that if someone winds up just like the cat, then they certainly must have had a curious disposition. The consequent might have been produced by another antecedent.

> *'If you're curious, then you'll wind up just like the cat'*

is not a statement of equivalence.

The statement of equivalence

> *'If you're curious, then and only then will you wind up just like the cat'*

could be nothing other than a false statement.

There are two correct forms of inferences based on the implication relation:

1. If I assume that *'if p, then q'*, and I also assume that *p*, then I can infer *q*. This type of argument is known as the **affirmative mode** or, in Latin, the **modus ponens syllogism**, since here we inferred the consequent from the affirmation of the antecedent. To put it into schema:

$$p \rightarrow q$$
$$p$$

Therefore: q

2. If I assume that *'if p, then q'* and I assume that *q* doesn't hold *($\bar{q}$)*, then I can infer the negation of the antecedent from the negation of

the consequent. This is the **negative mode**, in Latin, **modus tollens syllogism**. The formula:

$$p \rightarrow q$$
$$\overline{q}$$

Therefore; $\overline{p}$

It's incorrect to infer the negation of the consequent $(\overline{q})$ from the negation of the antecedent $(\overline{p})$, or to infer the antecedent (p) from the affirmation of the consequent (q).

I'll give you examples for both the affirmative and negative modes:

Let's say that you're positive that if there's a red peg in the first peg-hole, then there's a green peg in the second peg-hole. After seeing the next row you know that there's a red peg in the first peg-hole. Now you can be positive that there's a green peg in the second peg-hole.

Now let's say that you assume that the proposition 'If it rains the street will get wet' is true. In this case if you look out the window and see that the street isn't wet, then you can infer the truth of 'It's not raining'."

"But what happens if it rains and the street still doesn't get wet because they covered it with a big tarpaulin?"

"Then this proves that your initial assumption (if it rains, the street will get wet) wasn't true. This doesn't change the correct nature of your argument. You're only guaranteed true conclusions by inferring from true premises."

"Inferences often come in handy when we want to make sure that the premises i.e. our assumptions we started from, are true. If we get as a conclusion a proposition which is obviously false by making a correct inference, then this just proves that one of the premises was false.

Now I'm going to tell you a story to see whether you've learned to make correct inferences:

> A women's dressing room was broken into sometime between 2 and 5 o'clock in the afternoon. The only door leading into the dressing room was blocked by a tough-looking woman security guard watching everything that went on. No man could have gotten in through the door during this period of time, even if he had been dressed up like a woman.

So if a man was the culprit, he must have gotten in through the window, then he must have left some evidence behind. He examined the window and found evidence.

Now hurry up and tell me what inference the detective was allowed to make."

"That the culprit was a man and he was skinny."

"That's the inference he was allowed to make, alright. It's just that it wasn't logically correct.

After deciding, our detective quickly phoned headquarters:

'Listen, Chief. A skinny man must have crawled in through the window. He's your culprit.'

His boss, who had already been filled about the details of the crime, replied:

'How many times have I told you, Sam, that you should study a little more logic. You're always jumping to conclusions.'

So the detective went through his line of reasoning one more time:
His inference (No. 1) was:

'I determined that there were fingerprints on the window, and since I knew that if the culprit had crawled in through the window he would have left fingerprints behind him, I was entitled to conclude from two premises that (therefore) the culprit had gone in through the window. The deduction I used is known as the modus ponens for stating conditional syllogism'.

Now you tell me, was the detective right?" - Agatha asked.

"No, he wasn't. He inferred from the affirmation of the antecedent. And anyway, the culprit could just as well have left fingerprints on the window if he had left through it."

"And would the inference still be correct even if there was no way that the culprit could have jumped out through the window?"

"No, it wouldn't have been correct then, either. Anyway, his initial statement wasn't that the only way the culprit could have left evidence was if he had crawled in through the window. The fact that the culprit climbed in through the window - whether or not it was true - simply doesn't follow from the antecedent the way the detective worded it."

"But our sleuth continued:
(Inference No. 2.)

> 'After I had decided that the culprit had crawled in through the window - and since I had previously determined that if the culprit was a man, then he must have crawled in through the window, I'm correct in inferring that (therefore) the culprit was a man. Once again I did this by virtue of the modus ponens for conditional syllogism."

"There goes Sam again," - interrupted John, "making another incorrect inference, and for the same reason as the time before. What did Sam say next? How did he decide that the culprit was skinny?"

"Sam proceeded along the following lines," - continued Agatha.

> 'If the culprit was a man, then he must have crawled in through the window, and if he crawled in through the window, then he was skinny, I can now get the conclusion that if the culprit was a man then the culprit was skinny. Furthermore, I know that the culprit was a man, so he was skinny. But what sort of inference was that? There must be a mistake here. I don't know the name of this form of inference.'

"Hey, Agatha! - interrupted John.
This same fellow must have studied about as much logic as I have. I don't know what they call this inferential form either - which wouldn't

be such a big problem, if I could tell you whether the inference was correct or not."

"Two inferences were made here. One of them we haven't talked about yet. This is **hypothetical syllogism**, otherwise known as a **chain inference**. If you know that an antecedent entails a given consequent and this consequent form is the basis of another consequent, then you are allowed to conclude that if the first antecedent holds, then the second antecedent must also hold. To put this in formula:

$$p \rightarrow q$$
$$q \rightarrow r$$

Therefore; $p \rightarrow r$

So Sam made the following inferences:
(Inference No. 3.)

> *'If the culprit was a man, then he must have crawled in through the window.*
> *If he crawled in through the window, then he must have been skinny.*
> *Therefore; if the culprit was a man then he must have been skinny'.*

This was a correct inference.
After this the next inference (No. 4.) that he made was the following:

> *'If the culprit was a man, then he must have been skinny.*
> *The culprit was a man, (I know this as the conclusion of inference No. 2) It follows from these two premises that the culprit must have been skinny'.*

This was another correct inference - a true modus ponens. The only problem is that one of the premises - the culprit was a man - was arrived at by incorrect inference. Since we can't really be sure whether the premises are true, we don't know whether the propositions, *'The culprit must have been skinny'*, is true either."

"Hey, Agatha! Do you know who the culprit was?"

"I haven't got the slightest idea. All we can figure out from these bits of information is that if he was a man, then he was skinny and left evidence behind on the window. But if the culprit wasn't a man, then there's no way we can go about getting new information."

"Gee, wouldn't it be good to see a pictorial representation of all this - maybe using the logic of electric circuits. But you don't seem to be interested in doing that at all - you aren't even curious. What I know simply doesn't interest you."

"Of course I want to hear. Go on and tell me all about everything you learned!"

The teacher's dilemma

John cleared his throat. Proud that it was finally his turn to be teacher, he boldly started the lecture.

"The first person to hint at the possible parallel between electric circuits and the laws of logic was the Austrian physicist Ehrenfest in 1912. Later, in the 1930's, Shestakov, a Russian logician, and Shannon, an American mathematician, arrived independently at the idea that the achievements of modern logic could be applied in solving problems of electric engineering.

It's a well-known fact that electric switches can be in an open or closed position. When they are closed, the electric current gets through (for instance, the lamp is on when the electric switch is turned on), while in the open position the current does not get through. So electric switches can be in two possible positions (open or closed), just as we ascribed two possible values (true and false) to propositions."

"So we aren't interested in how brightly the lamp is on, or how intense the current is. And the same thing is true in two-valued logic, where there is no such thing as 'maximally' true or 'minimally' true" - added Agatha.

"Right" - John concluded. "So now we can make the first comparison between logic and electric circuits. The closed (on) position of the switch can be likened to the truth of the proposition, while the open (off) position can be compared to the falsity of the proposition.

As you know, electric circuits may be connected in different ways. These ways of connection can be likened to certain kinds of compound propositions. Series connection is like a conjunctive proposition, while parallel connection is like a disjunctive proposition."

"Hold it a second. I don't know what series connections and parallel connections are. We might have studied that at school, but I can't remember."

"Alright, I'll draw them for you. First let's agree on using certain designations. We'll draw the switch like this:

We use this symbol when we aren't specifying whether the switch is in an open or closed position. To represent an open switch, we use the following symbol:

If the switch is closed, we represent it like this:

Now I'll draw you the diagrams for series and parallel connections. (The switches are marked with the letters A, B, etc.)

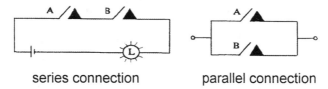

series connection   parallel connection

In a **series connection**, the current only reaches the lamps when all the switches (in this case A and B) are in a closed position. If either A or B, or both switches are open then the circuit is open."

"Now I see what they have in common with logic. The conjunctive propositions 'p and q' is true only when, p and q are true at the same time. But if either one of them or both of them are false, then 'p and q' is false, too."

"For the **parallel connection**, I'm not drawing the supply source and the lamp. The two rings of either side of the switch show that it's connected to the supply source and the lamps. As you can see from looking at the drawing, closing either one of the switches A and B is sufficient for the current to get to the lamps. The only time the lamp connected to the circuit is off is when both A and B are open. In that case the circuit is open."

"Draw me all the possible positions. I'll write down the corresponding compound propositions in logic. I'll use a **t** for true and an **f** for false."

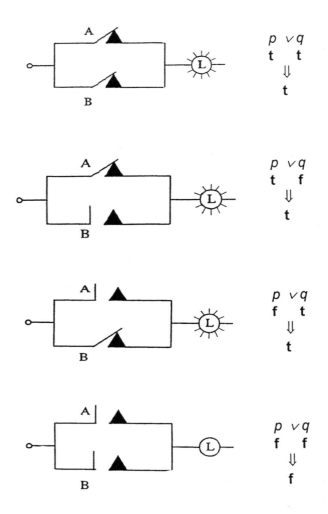

$$p \lor q$$
t   t
⇓
t

$$p \lor q$$
t   f
⇓
t

$$p \lor q$$
f   t
⇓
t

$$p \lor q$$
f   f
⇓
f

"You can also plan electric circuits which contain series connections and parallel connections at the same time. Tell me how you would write the corresponding proposition for this circuit:"

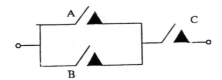

"*A or B and C.*"
"Now write that with symbols of logic!"

"*(p v q) ∧ r* We learned that parentheses play a very important role. Take the sentence '*Boating camp is open to anyone who is a member of either the rowing or sailing clubs, and is over sixteen years of age.*' This sentence can be interpreted in different ways, depending on where you put the parentheses. In the first instance, being over sixteen years of age is a prerequisite for being in boating camp. In the instance *p v (q ∧ r)* the requirement of being over sixteen years of age applies only to members of the sailing club."

"And how is negation interpreted with electric switches?"

"That's a cinch. If the two propositions are related so that one is the negation of the other, then this just means that when one of them is true the other is false, and vice versa."

"That's exactly right. And it just occurred to me how to define a pair of these propositions so that they correspond to the switches."

"Tell me, then."

"The way to make the two switches match a pair of propositions would be to have one in the closed position when the other is open, and vice versa. But how could we do that?"

"Well, we might try to link a magnet to the two switches so that when one of them is attracted towards the magnet, the other is repulsed ..."

"I don't get you there."

"Don't worry about the technical part of the problem. Instead, I'll just draw you two circuits where one is the negation of the other.

A   Ā

The dotted lines show a connection between switches A and Ā where if A is closed then Ā is open, and if A is open then Ā is closed."

"So far so good. But what happens when I want to put two switches inside the circuit where one is the negation of the other?"

"That depends on whether you're talking about parallel or series connection. If we install two of these switches parallel to each other, then the circuit will always be closed."

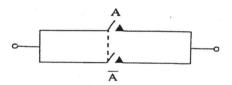

"Why's that?"

"Don't you get it?' I'll draw you the different possible variations:"

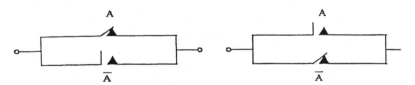

"Wow, that's really interesting! Why, of course! The disjunction $p \vee \overline{p}$ is true no matter what. The statement

'John is a good teacher or John isn't a good teacher'
is always true."

"Thanks a lot. Conclusions like that one will do me a whole lot of good. Your statement isn't worth ten cents, since it doesn't tell me what you really think about me."

"That's just the idea. Propositions which are always true are known as **tautologies**."

"You can go on and just get rid of those tautologies. They won't make you any smarter."

"Alright, don't be so edgy. Don't you see I only meant that as an example? I only mentioned that compound proposition for demonstration purposes. Now go on and tell me the rest of what you had to say."

"If we connect switches A and $\bar{A}$ in series, then the electric current will always be open.

As a tribute to your technical genius, I'll draw you the different possible solutions."

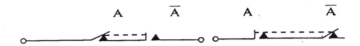

"Wow: The conjunction $p \wedge \bar{p}$ is always false. To affirm and deny the same thing can't be true at the same time."

"Wait a minute! Use the language of propositional logic to express what you just said in the last sentence "

"That's a breeze!

$$\overline{p \wedge \bar{p}}$$

In other words $p \wedge \bar{p}$ are not true. But why did you ask me to do that?"

"Now I wanted you to ask me how to express the collective negation of several propositions with electric circuits."

"That's not hard at all. We already discussed that if $p \vee q$ isn't true, then $\bar{p} \wedge \bar{q}$ is true, or to put in another way, $\overline{p \vee q} = \bar{p} \wedge \bar{q}$."

"Can you draw this identity using electric circuits?"

Agatha thought for a minute. She started to draw something, and then gave up.

"I'm not getting anywhere. Could you help me a little?"

"Only too glad. First draw the electric circuit $A \vee B$. Then draw an electric circuit connected in series where there are two switches. Take one of the switches in the series circuit and connect it with a broken line to the A switch on the $A \vee B$ circuit. Connect the other switch to the B switch with a dotted line."

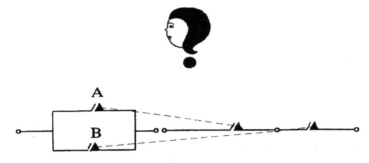

"In this case one switch of the series is $\overline{A}$ and the other is $\overline{B}$. Now how do these work?"

"When the series connection is closed, then both $\overline{A}$ and $\overline{B}$ are closed. But in that case, there's no current in the parallel circuit $A \vee B$

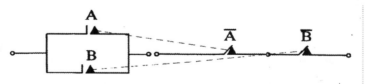

What this drawing actually shows is that $\overline{p} \wedge \overline{q}$ is true if and only if $\overline{p \vee q}$, in other words: $\overline{p} \wedge \overline{q} = \overline{p \vee q}$."

"Slow down! Don't go so fast. The only thing that drawing shows is that if $\overline{p} \wedge \overline{q}$ is true, then $p \vee q$ is false. You still have to show that if $p \wedge q$ is false, then $p \vee q$ is true, and that it follows from this that $\overline{p \vee q}$ is false. After you've proved that, then it is demonstrated that the value of $\overline{p} \wedge \overline{q}$ (whether true or false) corresponds to the value of $p \vee q$ in all cases."

"No sooner said than done. Here's the proof:

If the circuit $\overline{A} \wedge \overline{B}$ isn't closed, then either $\overline{A}$ or $\overline{B}$ is open, but in this case either A or B is closed. So the proposition,

'Its not true that A or B is closed'

is false.

I won't draw this since I think it's pretty clear already. I would rather like you to tell me why it would be worthwhile knowing that

$$\overline{p \vee q} = \overline{p} \wedge \overline{q}, \text{ or that } \overline{p \wedge q} = \overline{p} \vee \overline{q}?"$$

"Because then I could use the language of electric circuits to express implication, too. You're the one who pointed out that the truth value of $p \rightarrow q$ corresponds to the truth value of $\overline{p \wedge \overline{q}}$. So according to everything said already, the truth value of $\overline{p \wedge \overline{q}}$ corresponds to the truth value of $\overline{p} \vee \overline{\overline{q}}."$

"Right. And as I told you before, since the truth value of every even-numbered negation corresponds to the truth value of an unnegated proposition, then $p \rightarrow q = \overline{p} \vee q$. The circuit for the proposition $p \rightarrow q$ would look like this:"

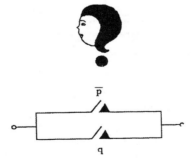

"I've also learned that any compound proposition can be expressed with either a conjunction and a negation, or a disjunction and a negation. For example, the truth value of p / q corresponds to the truth value of $\overline{p} \vee \overline{q}$. So now we know how to translate p / q in the language of electric circuits, too. But there's still one thing I don't understand. How do we use this entire comparison between circuits and propositions?"

"For one thing, we can use circuits to test the correctness of our inferences, and we can decide what conclusion will follow from given premises."

"Now that's really something. Let's see how that works."

"Well, I can show you how that inference you were speaking of in connection with disjunction would be correct. There we assumed the truth of $p \vee q$ along with the truth of $\overline{p}$, and then went on to make our conclusion. Translated to the language of electric circuits this would imply the following. There is a given electric circuit where A and B are connected parallel to each other, and where there is another switch working counter to the A switch which is connected in a series with the parallel connection.

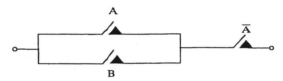

This electric circuit can only be in the closed position when the $\overline{A}$ switch and the B switch are closed. To go back to the language of logic, $p \vee q$ and $\overline{p}$ can only be true at the same time as q is true. So q actually does follow from the premises $p \vee q$ and $\overline{p}$."

"I can see how that's true, but it would be just as easy to understand, maybe easier, without all those circuits."

"Oh, you're just trying to egg me on. Everyone knows that it's not all that simple to use computers to solve rational problems. You're like one of those people who wonder why slide rules are so useful when you can figure out 2 x 2 in your head faster than on the slide rule. Or like someone who can't appreciate an airplane since it's faster to get to New York City by bicycle."

"Y'know what? Let's try a harder problem on your electric circuits. I heard a good riddle by the name 'the teacher's dilemma'. I really struggled to get the answer, and I'm still not sure whether I solved it correctly.

> The riddle has to do with a teacher who is grading students at the end of the year. She has to grade the students in relation to each other, and runs into problems, since she can only give one of five grades. She starts with the following statements:

I. *Edith is getting an A, or Bob isn't getting a B*

2. *Bob is getting a B, or Andy isn't getting a C.*

3. *Chester isn't getting a B, or David is getting a D.*

4. *David isn't getting a D, or Frank isn't getting a B.*

5. *Edith isn't getting an A, or Frank is getting the B.*

The problem is whether Andy would get the *C* and Chester the *B* if each of the above sentences is a true disjunction."

"And what did you decide?"

"That either Andy won't get the *C* or Chester won't get the *B*. In other words, the statements,

> *'Andy will get a C'* and *'Chester will get a B'*

can't hold at the same time."

"Well, let's see whether that's true. First let's start by writing the simple propositions so that we can talk about them a little more briefly."

"Okay. Let's do the formalizations like this:

Edith is getting an A	= *E*
Bob is getting a B	= *B*
Andy is getting a C	= *A*
Chester is getting a B	= *C*
David is getting a D	= *D*
Frank is getting a B	= *F*

In this case the five propositions are:

1. $E \lor \overline{B}$

2. $B \lor \overline{A}$

3. $\overline{C} \lor D$

4. $\overline{D} \lor \overline{F}$

5. $\overline{E} \lor F$

Let's assume that all five propositions are true, and see whether both A and C can be true at the same time.

Going back to switches, the question is whether the series connected made up of circuits 1-5 connected parallel to each other is closed when switches A and C are closed.

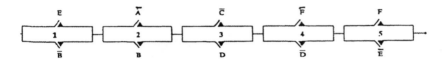

If switches A and C are closed, then $\overline{A}$ and $\overline{C}$ are open, so B on the second circuit and D on the third must be closed. But that would make $\overline{B}$ on the first circuit open, leaving E to be closed. On top of it, since D is closed on the third, on the fourth $\overline{D}$ is open and $\overline{F}$ is closed."

"Can the current pass onto the fifth switch?"

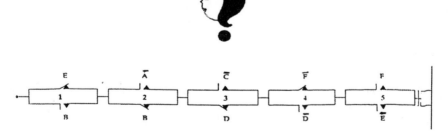

"No, it can't, since we know from 1 that $\overline{E}$ is open, and from 4 that F is open. "

o we've proved that if switches *A* and *C* are closed (in other words, if Andy is getting a *C* and Chester a *B*), then the circuit can't be closed."

I feel sorry for those poor kids. One of them is going to end up with a worse grade. But just a minute - we still haven't proved whether it's enough to say if only Andy won't be getting a *C*, then Chester can get a *B*, and vice versa. But now I can check this on my own.

Let's assume that if Andy isn't getting the *C* and Chester is getting the *B*, then the following situation will arise:

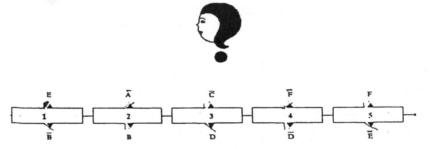

In other words, if Andy isn't getting a *C*, then

> Edith isn't getting an *A*
> Bob isn't getting a *B*
> David is getting a *D*
> Frank isn't getting a *B*"

"This would be another possible solution. But now only Chester stands to benefit. On top of it, David is even going to flunk. Now let's try the other possibility where Andy is getting the *C* and Chester isn't getting the *B*."

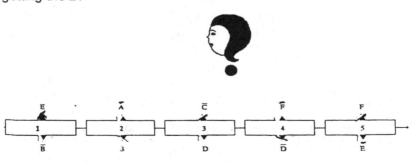

"This time:

Edith is getting the A
Bob is getting the B
David isn't getting the D
Frank is getting a B"

"If I were the teacher I'd solve the problem this way. Now only Chester stands to lose, while the rest wind up okay, and nobody flunks."

"I hope the teacher thought the same as you do."

"Say, Agatha, - do you know what the word 'dilemma' means? What does it mean to say, 'the teacher's dilemma'?"

"Haven't you ever heard anybody say, 'I'm in a dilemma - I don't know what to do'?"

"Of course I have. I've even used it myself. Once I was in a dilemma over whether to go to the beach with you or to go to the field to practice football. How am I supposed to use the word, anyway? I still can't figure out what a dilemma is."

"I know what it is since I looked up the etymology in the dictionary. And we studied about dilemma in logic. **'Dilemma'** comes from Greek. It means a forced, unpleasant situation which prompts the necessity of choice between two possibilities. The teacher had to choose between not giving Andy the C or not giving Chester the B. Now this teacher was very generous. If she had her way, she would have given everybody the better grade, but she also wanted to be fair. That's why she was in a forced, unpleasant situation - or as we say, in a dilemma
By the way, were you really caught in a dilemma over whether to come to the beach with me or go and play football? Why was that such a dilemma?"

"Well, if I had gone to the beach, then I couldn't have gone to play football; but if I had gone to play football, then couldn't have gone with you."

"Not another word. I already see what kind of dilemma you were in. You've just provided us with a handy example of inferences in the form of a dilemma."

"Gee, did I? What was the inference I used?"

"You recognized that one antecedent implies one consequent, and another antecedent another consequent. You were also aware that you had to choose one of the two antecedents. Knowing this much, you can always make the logical inference that you also have to choose between the two consequents. This inference can be expressed like this:

> *If I go to the beach, then I can't go to football practice.*
> *If I go to football practice, then I can't see Agatha.*
> *Either I go to the beach, or I go to football practice.*
> *Therefore; I either won't go to football practice, or I won't see Agatha.*

"Which one did you finally choose?"

"I went to the beach and got burned."

"Were you in the sun a long time?"

"No. The next day at the game, we got burned by the other team."

Prove that you are right

"Hey, John" - said Agatha. "Are you aware that we still have a debt to pay off?"

"Is that so? I forgot all about it."

"You certainly did. We still haven't shown how the example of the break-in can be represented in circuits."

"And all along I thought we'd borrowed money from somebody and not paid him back. I should have known that all you have on the brain is logic."

"Come on! Let's try then. I'll run through the premises and then find the formulae in the language of logic corresponding to the propositions.

> *'If the culprit was a man, then he crawled in through the window.'* $= p \rightarrow q$.
> *'If he crawled in through the window, then he was skinny.'* $= q \rightarrow r$
> *'If he crawled in through the window, then he left some evidence on the window.'* $= q \rightarrow z$
> *'He left some evidence on the window.'* $= q \rightarrow z$

Assuming that these propositions are all true, do they entail the truth of p, q and r?"

"The disjunctions corresponding to these implications are in order:

$$\bar{p} \vee q$$

$$\bar{q} \vee r$$

$$\bar{q} \vee z$$

The parallel connections corresponding to the disjunction have to be connected in a series (since they all have to exist simultaneously), and the z switch also has to be hooked on in a series.

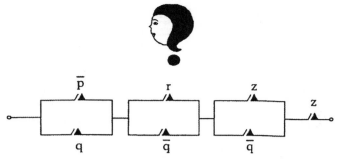

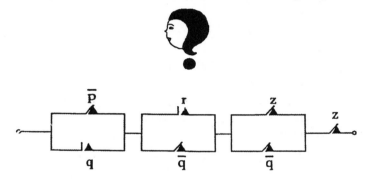

The circuit can be closed for example, in the following way:

In other words, if the premises are true you can also have a situation where the culprit was not a man, he didn't get in through the window, and he wasn't skinny. This is how we proved that Sam inferred incorrectly."

"I would also like to try to prove the hypothetical syllogism. The formula looked like this:

$$p \rightarrow q$$
$$q \rightarrow r$$
Therefore; $\quad p \rightarrow r$

First, I' ll change them into disjunctions:

$$\overline{p} \vee q$$
$$\overline{q} \vee r$$
Therefore; $\quad \overline{p} \vee r$

The circuit corresponds to the premises as follows:

"From this it certainly follows that $p \rightarrow r$, since either q or $\bar{q}$ must be open. So for the current to flow, either at least switch $\bar{p}$ or r has to be closed."

Agatha looked around John's room and said:

"What are all these books and crumpled papers doing on the floor? What were you doing?"

"You won't believe it" - John answered "I'm working on problems in logic."

"That's unbelievable enough. If I'm seeing right, these books are all poetry. Where did you get the logical problems from?"

"I invented them myself. I was not in the mood to read any of the books I have at home. I was bored. I thought of you, and naturally, that made me think of logic. I thought that by the time you get here I will think up some logical problems that you won't find so easy to solve either."

"You are really sweet. And did you succeed?"

"I think so. But see it for yourself. First I will read parts of poems for you. They contain compound propositions. Some of them are compounded of more than two propositions. Let's try and find out how to interpret them correctly."

John picked up a volume of poems by M. Babits off the floor and read:

"Words have become unfaithful to me by now, or I have become, like a steam overflowing its bed, hesitant, aimless shoreless..."

What is the role of the 'or' here?

"In my opinion it is a disjunction. The poet wants to say that one of two possibilities exist:
1. Words have become unfaithful to him,
2. He had become hesitant, aimless and shoreless himself. But I do not believe that these two possibilities are mutually exclusive. It's possible that words have become unfaithful to him and at the same time he has become hesitant."

"What do you mean by 'in my opinion'? Are you not sure of it?"

"I am sure that if M. Babits meant these lines the way I interpret them, then the logical form of his thought is disjunction. But no one can prove that such were his thoughts. It is only possible to advance arguments that make it probable that these were his thoughts."

"'Proof', 'arguments that make a truth probable' ... Do you want to know what I think if these? This: My friend, you are not going to interrupt me! First you solve my problems, then it will be your turn again!

Next follows an excerpt from A. József:

> 'If you strike blows all around destiny
> the elite wasteland breaks out in screams-
> the wide bladed axe is smiling.'

How would you express this in the terminology of logic?"

"$p \rightarrow (q \wedge r)$"
"Why did you place your brackets like this, why not like:

$$(p \rightarrow q) \wedge r?"$$

"Because the latter would mean that the wide-bladed axe is always smiling, independent of what happens with the elite wasteland, whether it screams or not. But this is not what the poem is saying, it says that from a single base two resultant follow; *q* and *r*."

"I must acknowledge that your arguments have convinced me."

"Do you know what such arguments are called?"

"No, I don't know."

"Aren't you interested?"

"Let's say I am. Tell me quickly!"

"When you want to prove that your statement is true, you can do it by showing that it follows logically from statements that have already been accepted to be true. This is called direct proof. But you can provide proof by showing that the opposite is impossible. This is one of the methods of **indirect proof**.

Here two statements have been opposed:

1. One of it is expressed in logical terms as follows:

$(p \rightarrow (q \land r)$

2. The logical form of the other statement is:

$(p \rightarrow q) \land r$

You too agree that either 1 or 2 is the case. I have proven the truth of 1 by showing that 2 is false because it leads to an impossible consequence. Thus 1 is true."

"You have put over me again! But I will not give in! I will now read an excerpt from Ady:

'If we will die, we will die,
and if we die, everything that is here will be dead.'

Please, designate the composing propositions by letters, and tell me how you would represent these lines by Ady in logical terms."

"'We will die' = p
'Everything that is here will be dead' = q

$(p \rightarrow p) \land (p \rightarrow q)$

"And, at last some more lines by Ady:

'Hungarian words will either acquire new meaning or the sad Hungarian life will remain as before.'

"At last an exclusive disjunction! Both part of it together cannot be true, but one of them has to be true. Otherwise this compound statement is not true. It means; if Hungarian words acquire new meaning, than the sad Hungarian life will not remain as it was before; and if Hungarian words do not acquire new meaning, than the sad Hungarian life will remain as before."

"Wait, you don't know what an important discovery I have made upon hearing your explanation. You expressed Ady's exclusive either-or statement in the form of implication and conjunction."

"Did I? How?"

"Listen:

'If Hungarian words acquire new meaning, than the sad Hungarian life will not remain as it was before; and if Hungarian words do not acquire new meaning, than the sad Hungarian life will remain as before'."

"And what is your discovery?"

"I know how to express an exclusive disjunction by disjunction and conjunction.

The way you related the meaning of this Ady quote is as follows:

'Hungarian words will acquire new meaning' = p
'The sad Hungarian life will remain as before' = q

$$(p \rightarrow \bar{q}) \wedge (\bar{p} \rightarrow q)$$

We already know that

$$p \rightarrow q = \bar{p} \vee q$$

from this follows that

$$p \rightarrow \bar{q} = \bar{p} \vee \bar{q}$$

$$\overline{p} \to q = p \vee q$$

Thus, expressed by way of disjunction and conjunction, Ady's lines look as follows:"

$$\overline{(p \vee \overline{q})} \wedge \overline{(p \vee q)}$$

"Wonderful! Let's devise an electric circuit in association with the exclusive disjunction."

"As you wish. Here it is:

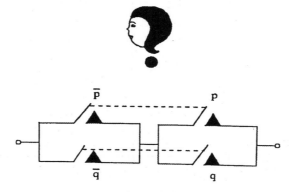

"When will be this circuit closed?"
"Can't you see it?"
"No, I can't."
"Look here! There are two possibilities for closing the circuit:"

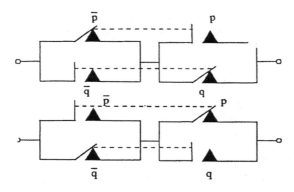

"I see, this is really what we state in the form of an exclusive disjunction. One and only one of the component propositions is true. At this moment Agatha noticed the Mastermind board in John's room. This is how the board was set up:

5	X X. O O	Y	B	G	V
4	O O	R	G	B	P
3	O O O	B	R	Y	G
2	O O X	G	P	V	B
1	X O	P	Y	G	R

"Why isn't the game finished?" asked Agatha.

"It was finished. But I took off the last row. I'd like you to finish it, but only after you've checked my inferences. I was playing this round with my sister, Ann. As you can see, after the fifth row I had my four colors. I just didn't know where they belonged. In the sixth row - the one I've removed - I put on the only possible solution. I've written down some of the inferences I made after the fifth row. Write them down in their logical forms, and tell me what type of inferences they are:

1. *G is neither in the second nor the fourth position.*
   If G is neither in the second nor the fourth position,
   then G must either be in the first or the third position.
Therefore; G is in the first position or the third position.

    2. *If G is in the first position, then B is either in the*
       third position or the fourth position.
       B is neither in the third nor the first position.
Therefore; G isn't in the first position.

    3. *G is either in the first position or the third position.*
       G isn't in the first position.
Therefore; G is in the third position.

    4. *Either B is in the fourth position, or V is in the third*
       position.
       V isn't in the third position.
Therefore; B is in the fourth position."

Agatha then wrote down the logical forms of the inferences:

    1. $\bar{p} \wedge \bar{q}$
       $(\bar{p} \wedge \overline{q}) \rightarrow (r \vee z)$
Therefore; r ∨ z

    2. $p \rightarrow (q \vee r)$
       $\bar{q} \wedge \overline{r}$
Therefore; p

    3. $p \nabla q$
       p
Therefore; q

    4. $p \nabla q$
       q
Therefore; p

After the list was ready she said:
"I didn't run into any difficulties with the third and fourth inferences. Both were correct on the basis of exclusive disjunction. But I had to spend a lot more time thinking about the first two inferences. Then I realized that both were conditional syllogisms. The first was the modus ponens, while the second was the modus tollens. The odd

thing about this was that the antecedent and consequent are in themselves compound propositions made up of two propositions.

In number 1. the antecedent is $p \wedge q$. From the affirmation of it we can infer the affirmation of the consequent $(r \vee z)$.

In number 2. the consequent is $q \vee r$. We use the negation of this - in other words, $\overline{q \vee r}$, or $\overline{q} \wedge \overline{r}$, which are identical in value - to conclude the negation of the antecedent $(\overline{p})$."

"So have you figured out what was in the sixth row?"

"Just a minute, I still haven't decided. Your inferences were correct. So if your premises were true, then green was in the third position and blue was in the fourth position.

But where was yellow? I knew after the first row that yellow couldn't be in the second position, because we've only got one **X** key peg and that has to stand for the **G**. Wait a minute. I've got the hidden code! This is how I inferred the answer:

> *If Y isn't in the second position, then it must be in*
> *the first.*
> *Y isn't in the second position.*
> *Therefore; Y must be in the first position.*

Now write that down in formula form, John, and try to decide what type of inference I made."

"That's a cinch."

$\overline{p} \rightarrow q$
$\overline{p}$
Therefore; q

"That's the modus ponens for conditional syllogism."

"Doesn't it throw you off that I inferred q from $\overline{p}$? Would you still call that the modus ponens?"

"Why, sure I would. In the proposition $\overline{p} \rightarrow q$, the antecedent is $\overline{p}$, and we used it - in other words, we used the affirmation of the antecedent - to make our inference. But don't keep me in suspense. Tell me what the hidden code was?"

"Nothing could be simpler," said Agatha. And she put the sixth row on the game board.

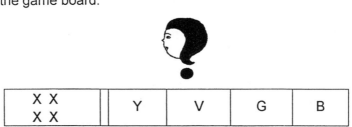

X X X X		Y	V	G	B

"That's right. That's the solution, " - said John.

"Are you sure that was the only choice possible? Can you prove that this was the only possible hidden code?"

"To prove, to prove! I have no idea whether it was acceptable as proof according to logic. What a terrible thing it would be if people had to prove every statement they made. But I admit that it's often important to be able to prove the truth of some statement, and that it comes in handy to know when a statement can be called proven. Now here's your chance to talk about proof! I would appreciate it if you could sum up everything I should know on the subject."

"Proven truths are statements where we can show that their truth can be inferred logically and correctly from other truths or axioms which have already been proven."

"What I don't understand is that these 'other already proven truths' had at one time to be proven. They had to be inferred from other already proven-truths. But this would lead to an infinite series. Where is the end? Can everything be proven by this method?"

"Not everything. In every branch of science - since this is where proof plays an especially important role - there are statements which are accepted as the outcome of proven truths. These statements are known as **axioms**. Theorems are generally selected to be axioms when their truth is visible by direct observation, and is justified by the practical experience of many centuries."

"Well, that's reassuring. People could very well accept for centuries as true something that is actually false. Direct observation can be misleading."

"You have a point there. But the situation doesn't have to be all that disturbing. Axioms are also proved by the fact that the system of theorems which has been derived from them works well in experience. Theorems accepted as scientific truths rarely turn out to be completely false. They usually just turn out to be valid over a more restricted area than what was formerly believed. Or sometimes they may only turn out to be true when viewed alongside given criteria - the need for which was previously not known."

"I believe that in these cases we may speak of faulty process of proof. Right?"

"Well, yes. This is a mistake connected with arguments. **Mistakes in proof** can be divided into two main groups. The first group is made up of potential mistakes in logic which come up during the process of proof. These are mistakes in inference. Proof occurs in the form of inferences. **Arguments** advanced in support of the evidence are the premises of deduction, and the inferred conclusion is itself the theorem which has to be proven. If the deduction is logically incorrect, then it makes no difference whether the arguments are true, the truth of the conclusion still hasn't been proved. These mistakes are known as formal mistakes in proof.

The second group is made up of mistakes connected with **demonstrative arguments**. The most common example of this is the use of the false argument. The theorem advanced as an argument may still be a true statement. It's just that in the given case it has been **under-proven** as an argument. To this category belongs the problem we were just talking about, where the argument can't be applied to the proof of the whole theorem. You remember the proof for 'B is in the fourth position'. When we were discussing Mastermind I told you that this statement can only be inferred from the statement, 'If B is in the fourth position, then we have to get the X markers in the second row' when we assume that G is in the first position. In this case the premise and conclusion are true, while the theorem is only proven in special cases - in other words, when G is in the first position.

Of course, the opposite of this mistake in proof can also occur when you use an argument which has been overproved. Here the arguments are overly generalized truths. They can be true in other instances over and beyond the theorem you are proving, and this makes them unsuitable for the proof in the situation precisely at hand. For instance there must have been a time when you were little when your throat hurt and you had a fever, and your grandmother considered this as sufficient evidence for you having snuck outside without your mittens on. A fever and a sore throat can be caused by many, many, other things, which means that outside the theorem to be proved (the fact that you snuck outside without any mittens), a lot of other things would have also been true."

"It must have been a very unhappy experience of your childhood that you still remember it. But you're wrong to think that I must have gone through the same thing. My grandmother is a pediatrician. Sorry, but this time you're the one who provided the sample of the mistakes in logic. You just used an argument which has been under-proved. The fact that some grandmothers get overly anxious doesn't necessarily allow us to make general inferences about all grandmothers. That's a false generalization."

"Okay, you win! And in refusing to accept without first considering what I, your teacher, told you, you've just demonstrated the application of another important rule in logic. This rule says that you shouldn't rely on somebody's authority or their good or bad reputation as evidence. Arguments which run, 'X made that statement, therefore it must be true because he should know' or 'Y said it, therefore it isn't true because he's someone you shouldn't believe' operate solely on the basis of authority or the lack of it. Proof that makes use of arguments like those is incorrect.

Never accept anything you feel to be important without first having stopped to think for yourself about whether it's really true."

IV.

Instead of epilogue

"What are you wrecking your brains over, Gabriel?"

"About a problem of logic."

"A problem of logic?"

"Yes or rather, over a riddle. I have the solution, but now I would like to translate it into the language of logic - Based on what we have learned. I would like to prove, using logic, that my solution is right. But I don't seem able to succeed."

"Let me hear that convoluted task."

"Listen! I am telling it!"

Who phoned Mary?

A female voice called me - says Mary - and was surprised that I did not recognize her voice, since the mother-in-law of her father is my mother. This made me wonder, because I am the only daughter of my parents."

"Well, who was the person who phoned Mary?"

"Her daughter, of course. I have solved that problem, but I am not able to reconcile it with what I have learned thus far."

"Be assured, the fault lies not with your equipment. Whatever you have learned thus far will not help you with solving this riddle (or, to be more exact, it does not help you directly). You would need to know other chapters of logic of which you haven't even heard yet. Up to know you have only studied some of the simplest logical procedures and deductions. You can not expect to be able to prove the correctness of the solution of any problem in logic on the basis of what you have learned thus far. This would be just as vain a hope as if you expected to read French literature in the original language after 20 lessons in French. But of course you wouldn't think 20 French lessons completely useless, would you?"

"No, 20 French lessons are only sufficient not be completely at a loss in that language."

"Perhaps it would be also sufficient to motivate you to further study that language. Well, this much was more or less the objective of the book '*It's Logical!*' to raise consciousness of the peculiarities of some simple logical procedures often applied in everyday life and to arouse the interest of the reader in problems of logic or philosophy."

INDEX

DATE DUE